D0936854

Dakar & West African Economic Development

DAKAR
and West African Economic Development

by Richard J. Peterec

COLUMBIA UNIVERSITY PRESS *New York and London* 1967

*Richard J. Peterec is Assistant Professor of Geography
at Bucknell University.*

Preface

THE FOLLOWING study is based on my interest in and research on West Africa over a period of six years and three field trips that have taken me to literally every country of the region. My first research trip was taken in 1960. At the time of my arrival early in that year, only Liberia, Ghana, and Guinea were politically independent; at the time of my departure, independence had come to Senegal and former French Sudan in the form of the now-defunct Mali Federation and to Togo; by the end of that year all the territories of West Africa were politically independent with the exceptions of Sierra Leone, the Gambia, and Portuguese Guinea. From the specific point of view of this study, at the time of my first arrival in West Africa, French West Africa was in the early stages of redefining and reshaping its future status. The concept of continued federation within a broader French Union was dead, and in its place had risen one completely independent state (the Republic of Guinea) and six semi-independent states closely associated with France within the newly created French Community.* By the end of the year, all eight territories of former French West Africa were completely independent.

With independence for most of West Africa (and especially for the new states of former French West Africa) came a modification in many of the economic and political ideas introduced to the region by the former colonial powers. In 1964 and 1966 I returned to West Africa to study some of these changes. More specifically in terms of this study, I returned to examine the effect that independence for the states of

---

* Although French West Africa consisted of eight territories, two of them, Senegal and former French Sudan, had united to form the Mali Federation on April 4, 1959.

West Africa and the introduction of a new set of international relationships has had upon one of these colonial legacies, namely the port of Dakar.

It should be noted that this is a study of the effect of independence upon the port of Dakar and not upon the city of Dakar in general, a distinction which must be emphasized. The city of Dakar, like most large, modern urban centers, is a complex and dynamic body which grew in response to countless forces. It had developed a series of functions in response to human needs in a particular society—a French colonial society embracing a large area of West Africa—which, at least since 1960, has witnessed a major political change. Under French colonial rule, Dakar emerged as the capital city of colonial French West Africa and the successor Federation of French West Africa, and as the largest city, the commercial hub, the leading industrial center, and the most important port in terms of tonnage handled of French-speaking sub-Saharan Africa. The purpose of this study is to examine and analyze only one function of the Dakar urban complex, namely its function as a port. More specifically, its purpose is to examine its function as a port in light of the recent political changes in West Africa. In doing so, and to understand fully the role of the port of Dakar within the political and economic framework of present-day West Africa, one must first look at the physical base, the historical development, and the political evolution of West Africa. Only then will one be able to understand fully the forces and factors which are in the process of shaping its role in the newly emerged political pattern of this region.

My reasons for making this study can be summarized very briefly: my great interest in tropical Africa (particularly French-speaking West Africa) and the help and encouragement of two American Africanists, Professor William A. Hance of Columbia University and Mrs. Irene S. Van Dongen. It is they who have helped my seed of interest in Africa to germinate and, hopefully, mature, and whose assistance, guidance, and perhaps above all, patience have led to the preparation of this manuscript. I am also greatly indebted to the Office of Naval Research, through whose generous assistance the preparatory work in the United States and France and the first field trip to West Africa were made possible. In addition, I am grateful to Bucknell University, Shell Com-

panies Foundation, Incorporated, and Delta Steamship Lines of New
Orleans, whose combined generosity enabled me to make the resurvey
of existing conditions during the summers of 1964 and 1966 and to the
many people in the United States, France, and West Africa who so
kindly and graciously assisted me in the collection of the facts and
materials necessary for the preparation of this study. And finally, it is
sincerely hoped that this study will contribute somewhat to a further
understanding on the part of interested Americans of that relatively
neglected—at least on the part of English-speaking people—area of
Africa so succinctly known as "l'Afrique francophone."

RICHARD J. PETEREC

Bucknell University
January 7, 1967

Contents

Dakar & West African Economic Development

Introduction

THE PORT of Dakar, like many other institutions introduced and developed during the colonial period, is in the process of having its role in independent West Africa redefined and reshaped. Since the political independence of Senegal, Mali, and Mauritania in 1960—or perhaps more accurately, since the first stages in the dissolution of French West Africa in 1959—a series of new political and economic relationships has been introduced in West Africa which, among other things, is in the process of modifying the traditional role of the port in this region. Some of these changes have come about suddenly and unexpectedly (for example, the political break between Senegal and Mali between 1960 and 1963 which forced Mali to develop new ties with other neighboring states, notably the Ivory Coast), while others have been and are being developed more gradually (for example, the political and economic relationship between Senegal and independent Gambia). Responding to these changes, the role of the port of Dakar within the institutional framework of West Africa today is different from what it was before the dissolution of French West Africa and substantially different from what it very likely will be in the future.

By 1958 the port of Dakar had grown from its original conception in the nineteenth century as a supplemental coaling station on the Europe–South America run to become the leading port of French West Africa, one of the largest ports of West Africa in terms of facilities, total tonnage handled, and areal extent of hinterland, and one of the world's foremost bunkering centers. In addition, the city of Dakar had become the largest city and capital of the entire federation and the leading commercial, industrial, and cultural center of French-speaking sub-Saharan Africa. Then, on September 28 of that year, the famous "de Gaulle Referendum" was held. Under its terms, the eight territories of French West Africa (as well as those of French Equatorial Africa, Madagascar, the Comoro Islands, and French Somaliland) were given the opportunity of choosing between immediate and absolute independence and one of three dependent relationships with France. With the single exception of French Guinea (now the Republic of Guinea), the territories chose, in ostensibly free elections, to become autonomous republics associated with France within the framework of the then newly born French Community. Guinea, in choosing immediate independence, was arbitrarily and unceremoniously excluded from the Community and from all economic rights and duties derived from the former federal relationship, although until her voluntary severance in March 1960 she did remain within the franc monetary bloc. However, within twenty-six months of the referendum, the seven remaining states, following the dictates of internal political expediency, had demanded and received from France the outstanding requisites for complete political independence, although they remained within a remodeled Community.[1]

With independence, a new set of forces was set into motion—a set of forces no longer centered at and controlled by Dakar but dictated by the wants and needs of each individual state. The concept of continued federation, even with independence, had been rejected in favor of individual territorial sovereignty. However, the attainment of political independence by these eight former colonial territories did not and could not mean the immediate abolition or complete modification of many of the numerous political, economic, and social institutions introduced and developed by the French during their more than fifty-year rule.

Although French West Africa was organized originally as a federation of a number of colonies each of which had its own colonial governor, the federation could not escape the strong control and centralization inherent in the office of the Governor-General resident in Dakar. This fact, coupled with the early creation of a single French West African economic and financial bloc, resulted in a unified plan of development for the federation as a whole, a plan which was followed by the French until their relinquishment of political and economic control. The unified plan of development resulted in considerable economic interdependence among the eight territories, often at the expense of sounder and more practical economic relations with other neighboring states. This interdependence becomes manifest in an examination of the patterns of internal and external trade, in a study of the establishment of industries, or in a survey of the currents of human migration. The recently established industries of the coastal states depend largely upon extranational markets, markets found to a large extent within the former federation. The climatic complement between the drier desert and sahelian zones to the north and the wetter tropical zones to the south calls for an exchange of their respective agricultural products. Human migration within the former federation has always been of prime importance to the economies of the receiving coastal states as well as to those of the sending interior ones. And finally, the importance of the maritime ports of Senegal, the Ivory Coast, and Dahomey as historically virtually the sole existing outlets for Mauritania, French Sudan (Mali), Upper Volta, and Niger as well as for their respective countries indicates the complementary nature of the former federation. The pattern was ruptured somewhat following Guinea's option for immediate political independence, although, fortunately, Guinea was perhaps the most economically independent of the West African territories.

A more serious modification of this induced interdependence of the states of former French West Africa came about after the rupture of the Mali Federation in August 1960 and the subsequent political and economic estrangement between Senegal and Mali. Coupled with Guinea's earlier separation from the Community, this decision resulted in the division of former French West Africa into two separate geographic blocs and in the reorientation of the traditional overseas trade pattern of Mali, much to the detriment of the Senegalese ports of Dakar and Kaolack. This rupture was healed, however, in 1963. Despite these two serious modifications of the traditional political and economic patterns, it must be remembered that, from the time of its creation in 1904, French West Africa had developed as an economic entity, the continuation of which was (and still is) to a very large extent necessary for the economic well-being of much of the area.[2]

Although independence for French West Africa has probably not yet brought about a substantial modification in the economic structure of the former federation, the future should witness a material change in this regard. The principal factors bringing about such a change are political and economic nationalism and the desire to reduce one state's heavy dependence upon another state. Guinea and Mali, the two prime examples, have already been noted. In addition, Mauritania is in the process of reducing her economic dependence upon Senegal; the Ivory Coast is rapidly developing a local industrial base often competitive with that of Senegal; Upper Volta and Ghana have made overtures (so far unsuccessful) to develop mutual ties; and Niger and Nigeria are in the process of developing new links. Thus the future will very probably witness a substantial reorientation in the economic and possibly political ties of these states.

One of the series of institutions introduced and developed by the French to serve the whole federation and which is in the process of adapting to the new political and economic realities is the system of maritime ports and servicing systems of hinterland transportation facil-ities. Its basic structure is already starting to respond to these changes. At the time of the dissolution of French West Africa, virtually all of the federation's overseas trade passed through its ports: Port Étienne in Mauritania; Saint Louis, Dakar, Kaolack, and Ziguinchor in Senegal; Conakry and Benty in Guinea; Tabou, Sassandra, and Abidjan in the Ivory Coast; and Cotonou in Dahomey (see Fig. 1). Lagos in Nigeria was perhaps the leading exception, although its percentage of the total overseas trade of the federation, whether measured in terms of volume or value, amounted to less than 1 per cent.

Today, while it is still true that most of the overseas trade of the Community passes through its ports, it is also true that new patterns are starting to emerge. In Mauritania the railroad from Port Étienne to Fort Gouraud has been completed, and, in addition to evacuating the Société Anonyme des Mines de Fer de Mauritanie (MIFERMA) iron ore, this port and rail line are used to supplement the port of Dakar as an outlet for the northern region of the country. Also, the wharf at Nouakchott was completed late in 1965 (though officially in-augurated in April 1966) with the intention of its eventually becoming, when a satisfactory road web is constructed, the principal port for

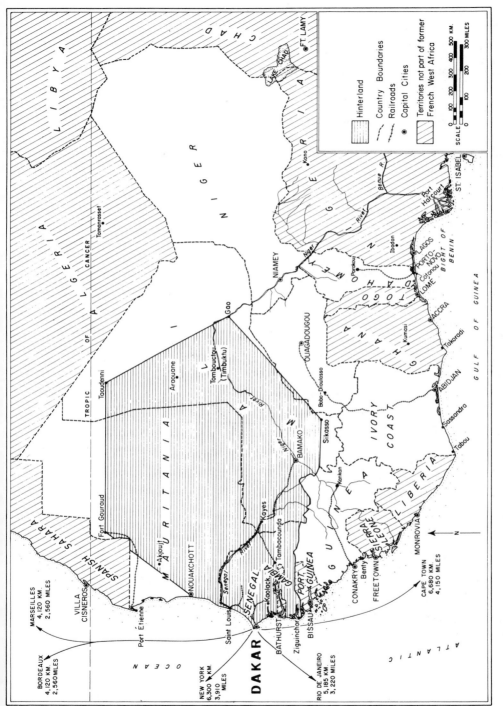

FIG. 1 West Africa showing the hinterland behind the Port of Dakar

central and southern Mauritania. In Senegal, Mauritania's economic nationalism will have, in the long run, a limited negative effect upon the port of Dakar. Also, the effect of a possible political and/or economic federation between Senegal and independent Gambia is under study. Mali, as a result of the 1960 Senegal-Mali rift, is in the process of developing supplemental outlets to reduce her former virtual sole dependence upon the ports of Senegal. In Guinea, Conakry and Benty are no longer within the Community, but, since these ports serve and have served only Guinean hinterlands, this has had no effect upon the other states of the former federation. However, the possibility of the construction of a rail line between Kankan or Kouroussa and Bamako in Mali, although remote at the present time, has not yet been definitely ruled out. In the Ivory Coast the booming port of Abidjan, while retaining most of the overseas trade of the Ivory Coast and Upper Volta, has captured some of the trade of Mali that formerly passed through Dakar or Kaolack, while a series of new wood-evacuation ports is being constructed along the developing western coast. And, finally, in Dahomey, despite the completion of the new deep-water port at Cotonou early in 1965, much of the overseas trade of landlocked Niger is being diverted from Cotonou to the ports of Lagos and Port Harcourt in Nigeria. Thus the traditional port and transportation pattern of former French West Africa is presently undergoing a change, the full ramifications of which will not be known until the passage of a sufficient length of time.

The port of Dakar is perhaps the best example in West Africa of a "colonial port" responding to the recent political and economic changes in the region. Not only is it the leading port of Senegal but also, in terms of total cargo and bunkering handlings, one of the leading ports of the West African Community (see Table 1) as well as of West Africa in general (see Table 2). It is a port that was founded and grew within a largely closed, centrally controlled colonial society that encompassed the bulk of West Africa. It developed a series of functions geared to a large extent to its role within such a community. The dissolution of French West Africa in 1959 and the subsequent independence of virtually all the colonial territories in West Africa have introduced a new set of relationships to which the port is in the process

TABLE 1   A Comparison of the Total Cargo and Bunkering Handlings of the Principal Ports of the West African Community for 1965
(In Thousands of Metric Tons)

Port	Embar-kations	Debar-kations	Total	%
Dakar	2,357	1,783	4,140	28.19
Abidjan	2,199	1,405	3,604	24.54
Port Étienne	5,979	52	6,031	41.07
Other Ports	637	272	909	6.19
Total	11,171	3,513	14,684	100.00

Sources: (a) Port Autonome de Dakar, Service des Statistiques, *Statistiques Comparées: Mois de Décembre 1965*, p. 2; (b) Files of the Ministère des Travaux Publics, de l'Urbanisme et des Transports, Dakar, Senegal; (c) République de Côte d'Ivoire, Ministère des Finances, des Affaires Économiques et du Plan, Direction de la Statistique, des Études Économiques et Démographiques, *Bulletin Mensuel de Statistique*, 19e année, No. 6 (Juin 1966), p. 6; (d) Files of the Service de la Statistique, Nouakchott, Mauritania; (e) Files of the Société Anonyme des Mines de Fer de Mauritanie (MIFERMA), Port Étienne, Mauritania; and (f) Files of the United States Embassy, Cotonou, Dahomey.

of adjusting. With the exception of sudden and unexpected events (such as the Senegal-Mali dispute), the nature of the colonial framework within which the port developed has precluded a sudden break with its past. As new relationships and values develop in West Africa, however,

TABLE 2   The Twelve Ports of West Africa With Total Cargo and Bunkering Handlings of Over One Million Tons in 1965
(In Thousands of Metric Tons)

Port	Embarkations	Debarkations	Total
Dakar	2,357	1,783	4,140
Port Étienne	5,977	52	6,029
Conakry			2,500[b]
Freetown	2,504	613	3,117
Monrovia	7,379	544	7,923
Buchanan	39	8,317	8,356
Abidjan	2,199	1,405	3,604
Takoradi	1,722	608	2,330
Tema	663	2,214	2,877
Lagos[a]	1,506	2,721	4,227
Port Harcourt[a]	701	821	1,522
Bonny[a]	7,353	—	7,353

[a] Figures are for calendar year ended March 31, 1965.
[b] Estimated total.

the role of the port in the region will be modified substantially. The purpose of this study is to examine and analyze the role of the port of Dakar within West Africa in light of these developing changes and to determine what its probable role will be in the future. To do this, and to understand better the forces that are in the process of shaping the future of the port within an independent West Africa, one must first have an understanding of the physical and historic forces that have conditioned its development and growth.

1 / The Physical Factors Conditioning the Development of the Port

BY THE beginning of the twentieth century the French had recognized the site inadequacies of Saint Louis and Rufisque as bases of operation for the continued development and exploitation of Senegal and the Senegal and Niger river basins. Being politically barred from the use of the Gambia River and its most favored estuary (except for two small peanut-evacuation points at Bassé and Saboya), they turned their attention to the then small coaling station of Dakar as the commercial heir apparent to the two larger settlements. The site of Dakar was (and still is) the only one along the entire Senegalese coast capable of being developed into a fine, modern port without the need of overcoming serious natural handicaps. Saint Louis,[1] Kaolack, and Ziguinchor, present-day secondary ports of Senegal, are seriously encumbered by shifting sandbars at the entrances to their respective channels which limit the maximum permissible drafts of vessels calling at the ports, by varying degrees of difficulty of navigation within their channels, and, in the cases of Saint Louis and Ziguinchor, by certain natural or political limitations to the extensions of their hinterlands. Rufisque and M'Bour, formerly important peanut ports of the colony, no longer serve in this capacity; neither possesses a natural harbor, their "ports" consisting simply of wharves projecting into the open sea. In Mauritania, Port Étienne offers natural site factors virtually identical to those of Dakar, but its location along the extreme northern coast of former French West Africa and its largely desert hinterland limited its development, until very recently, to a fishing and fish-processing center. Thus Dakar, taking advantage of a fine site and relatively good locational factors, developed into the leading port of French West Africa and its successor, the West African Community.

The Site Factor

It is along the coast of West Africa from northern Mauritania to the border of Guinea that past and future port competitors to the port of Dakar as the major drainer of the western Sudan[2] have arisen and might possibly develop in the future. This coast can be summarized as being low-lying, sandy, difficult to approach, and possessed of only three fairly good natural harbors: (1) Levrier Bay, the site of Port Étienne in Mauritania; (2) Gorée Bay, the site of the port of Dakar in Senegal; and (3) the Gambia Estuary, the site of the port of Bathurst in the Gambia. Other sites for port development exist, as is evident from an examination of the past and present-day port patterns along this coast, but serious natural deficiencies would make their development into major ports difficult without the expenditure of considerable effort and capital.

South from Cap Blanc Peninsula to Sangomar Point and the Saloum Estuary, the coast of West Africa quickly gives way from high cliffs along the extreme northern coast of Mauritania to a low, gently sloping, sandy shore, broken only by the volcanic basalts of Cape Verde Peninsula. In southern Mauritania and northern Senegal, thick coastal sand dunes are backed by interior wet depressions parallel to the coast. These remnants of former lagoons, known locally as "niayes," extend from Louga to Dakar. This smooth, even coast is the result of the interaction of the northeast trade winds, the southward-flowing Canaries Current, powerful waves, and tides. This combination of factors has produced the famous sandbar at the mouth of the Senegal River and the less well-known one across the Saloum Estuary, making penetration of these two channels by deep-draft ships very difficult and dangerous. Only the protected sites of Gorée Bay (protected by Cape Verde Peninsula) and Levrier Bay (protected by Cap Blanc Peninsula) have escaped the effects of this advancing sand. Thus, port development along this stretch of the coast has been limited historically to the two protected bays, the estuaries of the Senegal and Saloum rivers, and open wharves. Port Étienne has suffered because of its location (see above), while Saint Louis and Kaolack have found it difficult to overcome the limitations imposed by the sandbars across the mouths of their respective rivers. In addition, the costs and difficulties of operation at unprotected open wharves (such as the former wharves at Rufisque and M'Bour and the new wharf at Nouakchott) have precluded and will preclude their development into major "ports." Consequently, it was natural that Dakar emerge as the major port along this stretch of the West African coast.

The port of Dakar is situated on Cape Verde Peninsula, the westernmost protrusion of continental Africa. This peninsula, which extends 56 kilometers into the Atlantic Ocean from its continental base, resembles a huge east-west oriented crocheting needle with its hook pointing south (see Fig. 2). Geomorphologically, the peninsula is a tombolo, with the Miocene and Quaternary basalts of the triangular western platform (Cape Manuel, the Mamelles, and Almadi Point) being connected to the mainland by Quaternary sands. The government buildings, many fine residences, and the fine shopping districts of Dakar are located on the extreme southern portion of the platform. To the northeast, this platform gives way to the recent sand deposits, part of which are occupied by the northern portion of the port proper. The port facilities are located on the eastern side of the southward protuberance of the peninsula on Dakar Bay, a small indentation of larger Gorée Bay. Thus the port is protected from the drifting sands of the Canaries Current by the rise of the basaltic platform to the west and southwest. In addition, the inner harbor of the port is further protected by the man-made North and South jetties which shelter it, respectively, from the prevailing dry northeast trade winds which blow from November to the end of May and the rain-bearing southwestern monsoonal winds which blow the remainder of the year. Therefore, contrary to popular belief, the harbor of the port of Dakar is to a large extent an artificial one, the natural site factors being insufficient to afford it complete protection; Gorée Bay is much too large to give adequate natural shelter.

South of the Saloum Estuary, the effects of the Canaries Current and the trade winds die out, as does the parallel coastal cordon of sand. In its stead, a drowned ria coastline extends from just below the Saloum Estuary to Freetown, Sierra Leone. This stretch of the West African coast is the famous "Rivières du Sud" region of West Africa, and includes the Gambia, the Senegalese region of Casamance, and Portuguese Guinea. Although one generally associates a ria coastline with good port potential, this, with the single exception of the Gambia Estuary, is not

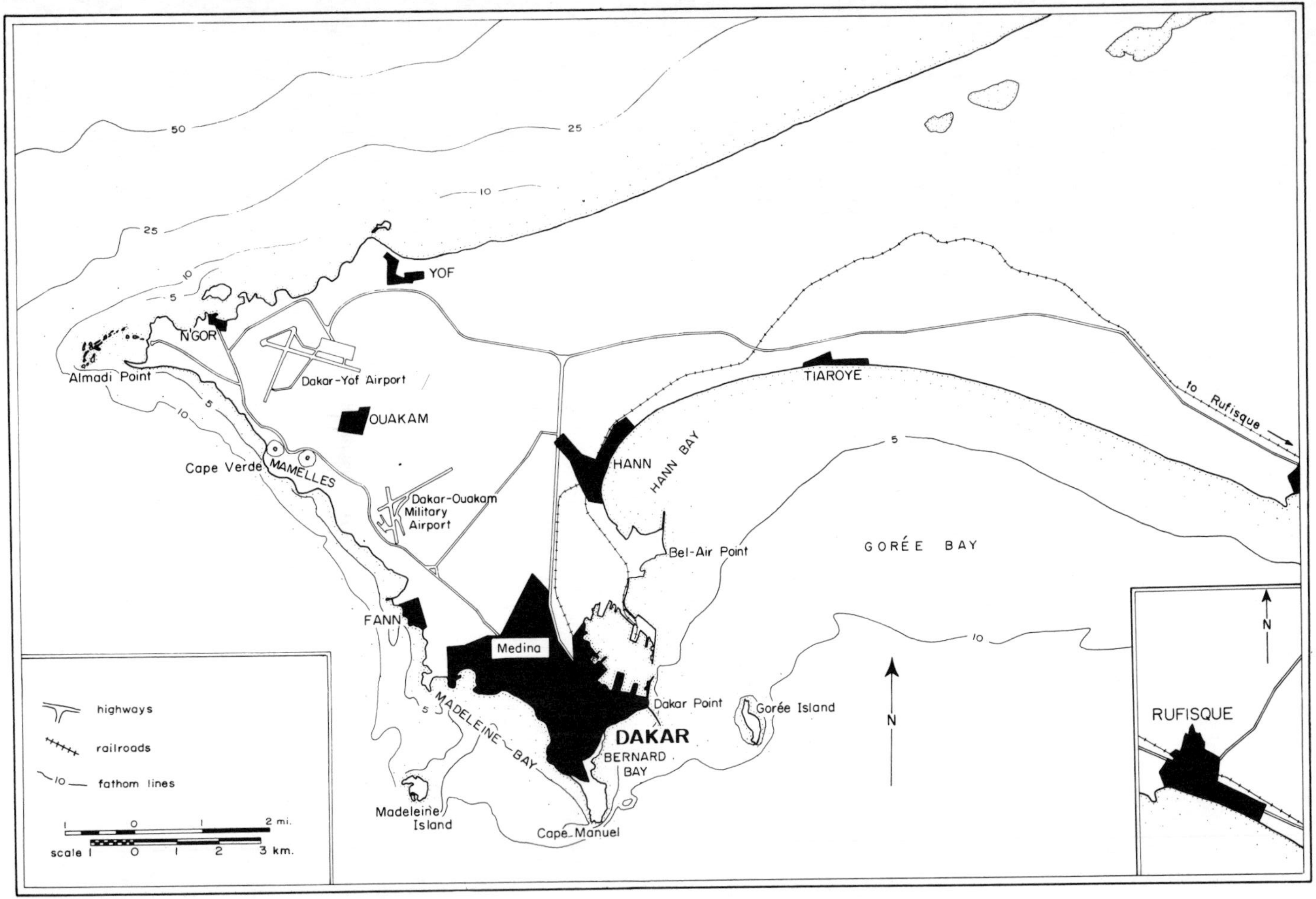

FIG. 2 Cape Verde Peninsula

true for the stretch of coast between the Saloum Estuary and the northern border of Guinea. An excessively high tidal range limits present use and future potential of the port of Bissau in Portuguese Guinea. In Casamance, the Casamance River, which to an unwary visitor to Ziguinchor appears to be a mighty tropical river, is in reality a small stream in an ancient, oversized valley invaded by the sea, the silting of which is prevented by the twice-daily scour of the tide. A small, shifting sandbar at the entrance to the main channel is the chief obstacle to deep-draft navigation on the lower course of this river. In addition, the Casamance Estuary is a confused, muddy labyrinth of mangrove forests and inhospitable swamps. The estuary of the Gambia River, on the other hand, has the site potential for development into a major West African port. Its port of Bathurst has no practical limitations on draft accommodations, is largely protected from winds and swells, and is backed up by the Gambia River, which is navigable throughout the year by ships of varying drafts as far as Koina, 470 kilometers upstream from its mouth. Unfortunately, British political control of this river until recently has precluded its full utilization as the natural outlet for the western sahelian and savanna region of West Africa.

Thus of the three relatively good sites for large-scale port development along the coast of West Africa between the northern coast of Mauritania and the border of Guinea, it is not surprising that Dakar alone developed into a major port; only Gorée Bay had the site requisites coupled with advantageous locational and political factors necessary to bring this about. Even if the future should witness the economic and political integration of the Gambia with Senegal, it is not very likely to have a strong negative effect upon the port of Dakar. Historical impetus plus the concentration of political and economic power in the Senegalese capital probably precludes such a development. However, the creation of a new "Senegambia" would almost certainly have a catastrophic effect upon the secondary ports of Kaolack and Ziguinchor.

The Location Factor

The second natural factor leading to the development of the port of Dakar is that of location: location with regard to principal Atlantic trade routes as well as to a relatively productive hinterland.[3] Its location close to the trade routes between Europe and southern South America first led to its selection in 1858 as a coaling station. Its strategic position at virtually the extreme western point of continental Africa coupled with its relative closeness to South America led to its development in 1898 as an important French naval base. Subsequently, the port's location near the Atlantic trade routes going from Europe to the west and southern coasts of Africa and from North America to the west, southern, and east coasts of the continent (as well as those going from Europe to southern South America) resulted in Dakar's development as one of the world's foremost bunkering and transit ports (see Fig. 1). The port has, with much truth, bestowed upon itself the title of "le Station-service de l'Atlantique." The importance of the port's bunkering function is readily apparent from the fact that in 1965 approximately 49 per cent of the total volume of cargo debarkations and 37 per cent of the total volume of cargo and bunkering embarkations (exclusive of water) were composed of petroleum derivatives.[4] To express these statistics in a more succinct manner, it could be noted that for the same year most of the petroleum imports were re-exported as bunker fuel. Dakar's role as an important port of call also has the positive effect of bringing in-transit tourists to the city, a total of 19,178 having debarked in the port in 1965.[5]

However, Dakar does not have the West African bunkering trade reserved solely for itself. Some competition comes from Freetown, Sierra Leone, favored by most British lines and others who prefer to buy within the sterling monetary bloc, but more serious competition comes from nearby Santa Cruz de Tenerife and Las Palmas in the Canary Islands. Because of their slightly lower prices (mainly because of lower social costs), a greater variety of fruits and vegetables for ships stores, a generally greater attraction to tourists, and a more direct location on the trade routes between Europe and South America, it is these two ports that present the strongest competition to the port of Dakar for the West African bunkering trade. Nevertheless, Dakar, owing to its superior loading equipment and ease of quayside access, manages to compete effectively with these ports by reducing the turnabout time with the consequent lowering of overall operating costs.

The location of Dakar in relation to the prevailing climatic, vegetative,

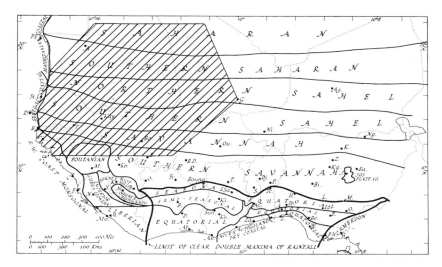

FIG. 3 The hinterland of the Port of Dakar in relation to the climatic zones of West Africa

Basic climatic map reproduced with permission from *West Africa: A Study of the Environment and of Man's Use of it* by R. J. Harrison Church, London: Longmans, Green & Co., 1963

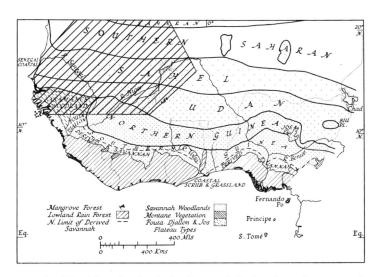

FIG. 4 The hinterland of the Port of Dakar in relation to the vegetative belts of West Africa

Basic vegetative map reproduced with permission from *West Africa: A Study of the Environment and of Man's Use of it* by R. J. Harrison Church, London: Longmans, Green & Co., 1963 and soil zones of West Africa is the second locational factor coloring and shaping the commercial pattern of the port. The port of Dakar is located on the west coast of West Africa where the coast cuts perpendicularly across the prevailing east-west climatic, vegetative, and soil belts (see Figs. 3 and 4). This, in turn, has resulted in a hinterland behind the port having an east-west grain parallel to these belts instead of perpendicular across them as, for example, in the port of Abidjan in the Ivory Coast. The net result is reflected in the agricultural mix of the non-bunkering embarkations at the port. In 1965 over 90 per cent of the recorded volume of agricultural embarkations at the port consisted of one basic commodity and its derivatives—the peanut (see Chapter 3).

For the purpose of this study, it is sufficient to divide West Africa into four climatic zones: (1) the desert, or Saharan, zone; (2) the semi-arid, or sahelian, zone; (3) the savanna, or Sudanese, zone; and (4) the humid equatorial, or Guinean, zone.[6] These zones can, if necessary, be subdivided into various subzones based upon various causal factors and local characteristics. In addition, since the nature and distribution of vegetation and soils are so mutually interwoven and tied in with climatic factors, the climatic, vegetative, and soil patterns can be examined together.

The northernmost climatic zone in West Africa is the desert zone which, in West Africa, is located entirely in Mauritania, Mali, and Niger. Approximately 40 per cent of the hinterland behind the port of Dakar lies within this zone (see Figs. 3 and 4). It is located north of approximately 18 degrees north latitude, has a very slight summer rainy season in the south giving way to no definite rainy season further north (although sporadic rains do fall), and has a large diurnal but moderate seasonal temperature range (see Table 3). Sparse xerophilous (drought-resistant) vegetation exists except where sources of underground water give rise to oases. The soils are generally stony or sandy and poor or lacking in organic matter (gray and red desert soils). These unfavorable physical factors give rise to a very sparse population (less than one person per square kilometer) and virtually no commercial agricultural production, a combination of factors having a strong negative effect upon port development (see Fig. 5). Only the discovery and exploitation of mineral resources, such as the copper deposits at Akjoujt and the

TABLE 3   Monthly Averages of Temperature and Precipitation for Two Selected Desert Stations in the Hinterland of the Port of Dakar

Fort Gouraud, Mauritania. Elev.: 297 meters 22°41' N, 12°42' W

	Jan.	Feb.	Mar.	Apr.	May	June	July	Aug.	Sep.	Oct.	Nov.	Dec.	Year
					Degrees C and mm								
Temp.	18.0	19.5	23.0	24.5	27.3	30.9	33.9	33.3	31.7	28.8	24.2	19.1	26.2
Ppt.	1	3	3	1	0	1	2	8	16	13	9	2	59
					Degrees F and in.								
Temp.	64.4	67.1	73.4	76.1	81.1	87.6	93.0	91.9	89.1	83.8	75.6	66.4	79.1
Ppt.	0.04	0.12	0.12	0.04	0.00	0.04	0.08	0.32	0.63	0.51	0.35	0.08	2.32

Araouane, Mali. Elev.: 280 meters 18°54' N, 3°33' W

	Jan.	Feb.	Mar.	Apr.	May	June	July	Aug.	Sep.	Oct.	Nov.	Dec.	Year
					Degrees C and mm								
Temp.	18.2	20.9	26.0	31.2	34.2	37.1	35.0	33.3	33.9	30.7	24.0	18.6	28.6
Ppt.	0	1	0	0	0	5	5	12	16	1	1	1	42
					Degrees F and in.								
Temp.	64.8	69.6	78.8	88.2	93.6	98.8	·95.0	91.9	93.0	87.3	75.2	65.5	83.5
Ppt.	0.00	0.04	0.00	0.00	0.00	0.20	0.20	0.47	0.63	0.04	0.04	0.04	1.66

Source: Modified from Frederick L. Wernstedt, *World Climatic Data: Africa* (State College: Pennsylvania State University), pp. 34, 37A.

iron ore at Fort Gouraud, both in Mauritania, can stimulate large-scale port development (see Chapter 4). However, although the relief generally presents little difficulty to internal transportation development, the factor of distance to the coast can present a serious and often insurmountable handicap.

The next east-west climatic strip to the south is the sahelian zone, which extends from approximately 13 degrees to 18 degrees north latitude and contains approximately 50 per cent of the normal Dakar hinterland (see Figs. 3 and 4). With the exception of the northern fringes of Nigeria, it lies, in West Africa, wholly within the West African Community. As the effect of the tropical high-pressure cell located over the Sahara is weakened, more total precipitation is received, ranging from approximately 125 to 500 millimeters in the northern sahel to 500 to 750 millimeters in the southern portion of this zone. Rainfall is highly erratic, and comes almost entirely in periods ranging from 2 to 3 months in the north to 4 to 5 months in the south. Yearly and diurnal tempera-

FIG. 5   Desert hinterland near Nouakchott, Mauritania

ture ranges are moderately high except in the immediate coastal region to the west (see Table 4). Vegetation becomes more dense, going from heavier grass in the north to open thorn woodland in the south, although the soils do not exhibit the serious leaching to be found further south (see Fig. 6). The light loamy or sandy soils are ideal for the production of millet (almost entirely locally consumed), which can grow with as little as 250 millimeters of annual rainfall, and the peanut (grown both for local consumption and as a commercial crop), which can be grown only in the southern, wetter portion of this zone and along the more humid coast. Other commercial crops are climatically limited to the relatively unimportant cotton and sesame (benniseed). Once again, the problem of transportation emerges as an inhibitor to port development. The bulk of this zone lies in the interior of West Africa, and virtually the only export crop, the peanut, depends upon inexpensive bulk transportation. Thus production is limited to areas near the coast and along or near the principal lines of communication. Fortunately, the marketing of peanuts takes place after the rainy season ends, thus enabling the full use of the limited road network. Unless future geologic prospecting turns up exploitable mineral deposits and/or diversification to other commer-

TABLE 4   Monthly Averages of Temperature and Precipitation for Two Selected
Sahelian Stations in the Hinterland of the Port of Dakar

Dakar, Senegal. Elev.: 37 meters 14°40' N, 17°26' W

	Jan.	Feb.	Mar.	Apr.	May	June	July	Aug.	Sep.	Oct.	Nov.	Dec.	Year
					Degrees C and mm								
Temp.	22.5	22.4	22.7	23.0	23.9	26.9	27.7	27.5	27.9	28.3	26.7	23.9	25.3
Ppt.	1	1	0	0	1	16	81	245	146	42	3	4	540
					Degrees F and in.								
Temp.	72.5	72.3	72.9	73.4	75.0	80.4	81.9	81.5	82.2	82.9	80.1	75.0	77.5
Ppt.	0.04	0.04	0.00	0.00	0.04	0.63	3.19	9.65	5.75	1.65	0.12	0.16	21.26

Tombouctou (Timbuktu), Mali. Elev.: 269 meters 16°46' N, 3°01' W

	Jan.	Feb.	Mar.	Apr.	May	June	July	Aug.	Sep.	Oct.	Nov.	Dec.	Year
					Degrees C and mm								
Temp.	22.2	25.1	28.3	31.5	34.3	34.0	31.3	29.3	31.1	31.5	28.3	23.1	29.1
Ppt.	0	0	0	1	3	21	59	80	45	2	0	0	201
					Degrees F and in.								
Temp.	72.0	77.2	82.9	88.7	93.7	93.2	88.3	84.7	88.0	88.7	82.9	73.6	84.4
Ppt.	0.00	0.00	0.00	0.04	0.12	0.83	2.32	3.15	1.38	0.08	0.00	0.00	7.91

Source: Modified from Frederick L. Wernstedt, *World Climatic Data: Africa* (State College: Pennsyl–
vania State University), pp. 36, 37B.

cial crops is successful, the peanut will very probably play the para-
mount role in the commercial activity of the sahelian zone.

Moving one climatic zone further south and coming closer to the
Gulf of Guinea, one comes to the savanna zone. This zone extends from
the southern limit of the sahelian zone, which passes through central
Senegal, southern Mali, northern Upper Volta, and southern Niger, to a
very uneven southern boundary passing through the center of the states
bordering on the Gulf of Guinea (see Figs. 3 and 4). It should be emphasized that the lines of demarcation between these zones are not fast
and sure, but are somewhat arbitrary, and that the transition from one
to another is gradual and not abrupt. The savanna region shows a continuation of the pattern set thus far: higher total precipitation spread
out over a longer rainy season, ranging from 750 millimeters spread out
over a 5-month rainy period in the north to approximately 1,250 millimeters spread out over a 7- to 10-month rainy season in the south. Varia-
bility of rainfall is less than it is further north, and relative humidity

FIG. 6   Sahelian hinterland near Saint Louis, Senegal

is generally higher. Seasonal and diurnal (especially in the rainy season) temperature variations are also less (see Table 5). Vegetation also continues the familiar pattern of becoming more dense as one moves further south, containing species from the dense tropical forests as well as from the drier north (see Fig. 7). With the heavier rainfall, leaching of the soil begins to become a serious problem, particularly in the wetter south. This is a densely populated region of West Africa with a greater variety of agricultural crops, although in terms of commercial production the peanut is still by far the most important. Other fairly important commercial agricultural products are cotton, sesame seeds, and shea butter from the seeds of the shea tree (karité). In this climatic zone, however, as in the previous one, the peanut will very probably play the dominant role, at least in terms of agricultural exports.

The bulk of the savanna zone in West Africa lies closer to the Gulf of Guinea than to the western coast of West Africa. Thus most of this relatively productive zone escapes the attraction of the port of Dakar and the other ports of the west coast, the overseas trade of this climatic-

FIG. 7   Savanna hinterland near Bamako, Mali

TABLE 5   Monthly Averages of Temperature and Precipitation for Two Selected Savanna Stations in the Hinterland of the Port of Dakar

Kaolack, Senegal. Elev.: 6 meters 14°08′ N, 16°04′ W

	Jan.	Feb.	Mar.	Apr.	May	June	July	Aug.	Sep.	Oct.	Nov.	Dec.	Year
					Degrees C and mm								
Temp.	23.8	25.8	28.2	29.3	29.9	29.6	28.1	27.3	27.7	28.4	27.6	24.7	27.6
Ppt.	0	1	0	0	8	60	165	307	219	59	3	3	825
					Degrees F and in.								
Temp.	74.8	78.4	82.8	84.7	85.8	85.3	82.6	81.1	81.9	83.1	81.7	76.5	81.6
Ppt.	0.00	0.04	0.00	0.00	0.32	2.36	6.50	12.01	8.62	2.32	0.12	0.12	32.40

Bamako, Mali. Elev.: 331 meters 12°39′ N, 7°58′ W

	Jan.	Feb.	Mar.	Apr.	May	June	July	Aug.	Sep.	Oct.	Nov.	Dec.	Year
					Degrees C and mm								
Temp.	25.2	27.8	30.5	32.1	31.7	28.5	26.6	26.0	26.4	27.4	26.8	25.0	27.8
Ppt.	1	0	4	17	69	137	231	335	209	62	10	0	1,075
					Degrees F and in.								
Temp.	77.4	82.0	86.9	89.8	89.1	83.3	79.9	78.8	79.5	81.3	80.2	77.0	82.1
Ppt.	0.04	0.00	0.16	0.67	2.72	5.39	9.09	13.19	8.23	2.44	0.39	0.00	42.32

Source: Modified from Frederick L. Wernstedt, *World Climatic Data: Africa* (State College: Pennsylvania State University), pp. 36, 37A.

vegetative region draining largely via the ports along the Gulf of Guinea. Only approximately 10 per cent of the present-day hinterland of the port of Dakar lies within this zone. In addition, it is very unlikely that Dakar would drain much more of this region even if the internal political boundaries of West Africa should largely disappear and the port be allowed to drain from a hinterland not largely politically conditioned. It is even more unlikely that the final climatic zone to the south in West Africa, the Guinean zone, will ever fall even partially within the pull of Dakar. However, the transitional zone of western Casamance in Senegal does exhibit a modified Guinean climate and today falls within the Dakar hinterland (see Fig. 8 and Table 6).

FIG. 8   Modified Guinean hinterland near Ziguinchor, Senegal

Brief mention should be made at this point of the nature of the structure and relief of the hinterland behind the port of Dakar. As a general rule, West Africa consists of a smoothly eroded platform of Precambrian rocks with occasional granitic intrusions, approximately one-third of which is exposed. The remaining two-thirds is covered by Primary,

TABLE 6   Monthly Averages of Temperature and Precipitation for Ziguinchor

Ziguinchor, Casamance, Senegal. Elev.: 10 meters 12°35′ N, 16°16′ W

	Jan.	Feb.	Mar.	Apr.	May	June	July	Aug.	Sep.	Oct.	Nov.	Dec.	Year
					Degrees C and mm								
Temp.	24.0	25.3	27.1	27.7	28.4	28.1	26.7	26.3	26.8	27.5	27.1	24.4	26.6
Ppt.	1	1	0	0	11	121	351	556	357	155	5	1	1,559
					Degrees F and in.								
Temp.	75.2	77.5	80.8	81.9	82.8	82.6	80.1	79.3	80.2	81.5	80.8	75.9	79.9
Ppt.	0.04	0.04	0.00	0.00	0.43	4.76	13.82	21.89	14.06	6.10	0.20	0.04	61.38

Source: Modified from Frederick L. Wernstedt, *World Climatic Data: Africa* (State College: Pennsylvania State University), p. 37.

Secondary, and Tertiary sedimentary rocks, Secondary and later volcanic intrusions, and Quaternary sands. Within the hinterland, the exposed Precambrian rocks appear mainly in portions of Mauritania, with limited appearances in Senegal and Mali. Mineralogical prospecting is far from complete, but certain generalized facts are now fairly certain: (1) except for limestone near Rufisque, Senegal is virtually without local sources of construction materials; (2) there are no indications of exploitable coal deposits within this region; (3) except for several limited strikes in western Senegal, soundings for petroleum have met with no success; (4) fairly extensive phosphate deposits are found in Senegal; and (5) fairly large iron, copper, and manganese deposits exist, mainly in Mauritania and Mali (see Chapter 4). It should also be noted that the relief of the hinterland behind the port of Dakar is generally flat and monotonous, with a very gentle seaward slope. Minor local variations do occur where escarpments have developed in the sedimentary layers or where intrusive and/or extrusive volcanism has taken place, but these do not present very serious transportation difficulties, nor do they disturb the east-west belted pattern of climatic and vegetative zones.

Thus the physical environment has had both a positive and a negative influence in shaping and conditioning the developmental pattern of the port of Dakar. In positive terms, the port is situated at one of the three good sites for port development along the western (Sudanese-desert) coast of West Africa, is located at virtually the extreme western end of continental Africa in proximity to important Atlantic trade routes, and has fairly good access to its hinterland. The former enabled Dakar Bay to be developed into one of the finest ports of Africa; the second led to its emergence as one of the world's great bunkering centers. In addition, although there is no good natural river route into the Sudanese interior from Dakar (the Gambia River to the south is in independent Gambia while the Senegal River to the north has severe limitations to its use as a major transportation artery), there are virtually no physiographic limitations to the construction of roads and rail lines.

It is the nature of the Dakar hinterland, however, that was and is the principal limiting factor to past and future port development. Although the location is the better of the two possible sites for port development (of which the other is Port Étienne) along the western coast of former French West Africa, the bulk of the present-day hinterland lies largely within the desert and sahelian climatic zones, with only a relatively small portion lying in the savanna region. Yet it is this savanna zone and, to a lesser extent, the southern sahelian zone from which the port draws most of its non-bunkering embarkations and which consume the bulk of its non-bunkering debarkations. Thus, in terms of agricultural exports, port embarkations are limited almost entirely to the peanut and its derivatives. Only the discovery of exportable mineral deposits (such as the phosphates of Senegal) or the development of commercial irrigation schemes could vary the embarkation mix of the port to any appreciable extent. But even these would not necessarily have any effect upon the port: witness the discovery of the iron ore deposits at Fort Gouraud in Mauritania and the recent construction of the MIFERMA railroad and the mineral port at Port Étienne (see Chapter 4). In any event, the establishment and growth of the port of Dakar has been and will continue to be conditioned by its natural environment. Its importance, however, cannot be explained solely on these grounds; the present-day pattern was also conditioned considerably by the vagaries and accidents of history.

2 / The Historical Basis for the Growth and Development of the Port

LONG BEFORE the European made his first recorded appearance along the shores of West Africa in the fifteenth century, considerable contact existed between West Africa—particularly the central and western Sudan—and the Arab states to the north, an association which lasted until the disruption brought about in the nineteenth century by European penetration of West Africa from points along the coast. In exchange for textiles and miscellaneous European goods carried across the Sahara in caravans, West Africa sent out ivory, ostrich feathers, skins, salt, and slaves. It was during this period that Tombouctou (Timbuktu) made its legendary name, being, along with Gao, one of the two leading commercial centers of West Africa. However, while this overland trade with North Africa was taking place, the first of the two historical periods in the development of the port pattern of West Africa was beginning: the period of the establishment and development of coastal trading posts.

Historical Development of the Maritime Port Pattern of West Africa

The early history of European exploration of West Africa is very confused and uncertain. Some historians credit its discovery to early Genoese explorers of the thirteenth century; others credit it to early Dieppe mariners of the following century. It is known with historical certainty, however, that Portuguese explorers and traders began to arrive along the coast of West Africa during the course of the fifteenth century. Until the fall of Constantinople to the Turks in 1453, European traders were preoccupied with the Mediterranean-Middle East trade route to the Orient in the search for spices, perfumes, precious stones, and silk. With the subsequent closing of this route by the Turks to the Christian traders of Europe (chiefly Venetian, Spanish, and Portuguese), new trade routes had to be found. This task was undertaken mainly by Spain and Portugal. Spanish explorers went west, and to them fell the discovery of the Americas. The Portuguese headed south in their attempt to reach the East, the most immediate result of which was the exploration of the entire West African coast. The name of Vasco da Gama and his discovery of the all-water route to the Orient at the close of the fifteenth century is well known, but less well known are the discoveries of the earlier Portuguese explorers such as Gonzales, Nuno Tristao, Diniz Dias, and Alvise da Ca da Mosto who, by 1488, had discovered and explored the west coast of Africa as far as the Cape of Good Hope.

With discovery and exploration came the first Portuguese settlements in West Africa: Arguin, near present-day Port Étienne in Mauritania, settled in 1445 as a rest station on the sea route to the south, and Sao Jorge da Mina (Elmina) in what is now Ghana, settled in 1484 as the principal Portuguese trading post in West Africa. Ten years later, under the terms of the papal award in the Treaty of Tordesillas, Portugal was granted a monopoly in African trade, and, wherever economically feasible, numerous small coastal trading centers were established. However, owing to the greater emphasis placed upon the more lucrative trade with the Orient coupled with Portugal's political subjugation by Spain, the sixteenth century witnessed the decline of Portuguese influence in West Africa and the coming of the English, Dutch, and, to a lesser extent, the French. Emphasis was still placed on the securing of rest stations on the route to the East rather than in Africa proper, although during this period the list of coastally traded commodities grew to include gum arabic, ivory, ostrich feathers, gold, peppers, and slaves.

By the beginning of the seventeenth century, following the granting in 1588 of trading rights along the Gambia River to certain English merchants and the capture of Sao Jorge da Mina (Elmina) by the Dutch in 1595, England and Holland were firmly implanted in West Africa. The Dutch consolidated their position early in the century by the construction of a permanent settlement and fort on Gorée Island near Cape Verde Peninsula in 1617 and the capture of Arguin from the Portuguese in 1638. This event led to the establishment of a permanent gum-trading station at Portendick near present-day Nouakchott in Mauritania. Portugal was left with a few minor trading posts south of Cape Verde Peninsula in what is today Portuguese Guinea and along the Gulf of Guinea.

It was Cardinal Richelieu who, jealous of the inroads made by the English and Dutch in West Africa, suddenly introduced France firmly on the scene. Although private French companies had traded along the entire West African coast for over a century, it was not until 1626 that government-sponsored monopolies were introduced. These were similar in organization to those of England and Holland which were already well established. At the time, the Dutch were firmly installed from Arguin down to and past Cape Verde Peninsula (but excluding the hostile mouth of the Senegal River), while the English were in control of the Gambia Estuary. With the exception of a few minor English, Dutch, Danish, and Portuguese posts, the Guinea Coast was largely avoided at this time because of its difficult nature and the backing tropical rainforest. France filled the gap by establishing a settlement near the mouth of the Senegal River at Bieurt in 1638, a settlement which, twenty-one years later, was tranferred further upstream to a more favorable and more defensible site on the island of N'Dar, the foundation of the city and port of Saint Louis. This, however, was not enough for the expansionist Colbert (a successor to Richelieu), who decided that in order to secure a true foothold in Africa it was first necessary to remove Holland from the scene and for France to take her place. This was accomplished in 1677, with France occupying Gorée, Rufisque, Joal, Arguin, and Portendick. In addition, a trading post was established in defiance of England on the north bank of the Gambia River near its mouth at Albreda. Holland was thus largely retired from the West African scene, and France, for the first time, became a true West African power.

This first period in the history of the development of the port pattern of West Africa came to a close just after the beginning of the nineteenth century. From 1677 until then, the interests of France and England in the region varied directly with that of their respective successes and failures in the wars of Europe. In 1692, following the War of the League of Augsburg, France lost Gorée, Saint Louis, and Arguin to the English, only to recover them five years later under the terms of the Treaty of Ryswick. This was followed by sixty-one years of un-interrupted French rule over the then consolidated territory of Senegal, extending from Arguin down as far as Casamance (but excluding the Gambia) and up the Senegal River as far as present-day Bakel. Thus, the pattern for most of the following two and one-half centuries of French presence in West Africa was set: since the best and most natural route to the Sudanese interior was denied them as the result of English domination of the Gambia River, the second best had to do—the use of the Senegal River with an outlet at the poor and dangerous port of Saint Louis. France began the development of this river route at an early date—the fore part of the eighteenth century—in the hope of creating an economic outlet for the gold of Bambouk and the gum of the Sudan. This project was a great success, for along with the gold and gum arabic the Senegal River drained the other traditional goods of the Sudan: raw skins, beeswax, ivory, and, by now the most lucrative trade by far, slaves for the American market.

However, as the fortunes of war turned once again against France, her holdings in West Africa dwindled, and all of Senegal was lost to the English at the outbreak of the Seven Years War in 1758. Under the terms of the Treaty of Paris of 1763, Gorée was returned to France, with the English retaining possession of the two routes leading to the Sudanese interior—the Gambia and Senegal rivers. Then followed a series of political musical chairs: France reoccupied Saint Louis in 1779; the English occupied Gorée that same year; Senegal was returned to France by the Treaty of Versailles in 1783. The English captured Gorée in 1800, losing it four years later only to regain it within a year. In 1809 all of Senegal once again passed to the English who, being more interested in their bases in the Gambia and Sierra Leone, showed little interest. And finally, after the fall of the French Empire and the signing of the Treaty of Vienna on June 3, 1815, all of Senegal plus Albreda on the Gambia River were returned to France. Also, that same year wit-nessed the abolition of the trade in slaves. With this the first period in the history of the development of the West African port pattern drew to a close.

This early period had a limited influence on the future port pattern of West Africa. Interest centered chiefly upon the establishment of temporary coastal trading posts and, with the exception of the valley of the Senegal River, limited penetration of the Sudanese interior. The industrial revolution, with its heavy demand for large supplies of oils and raw cotton for the textile industry and its reciprocal search for markets, had not yet taken place in Europe. Consequently, trade was mainly for the limited supplies of low-volume, high-value luxury items such as gold, ivory, spices, skins, gum arabic, ostrich feathers, and slaves. For such limited trade, deep penetration into the interior and the establishment of expensive, permanent port facilities and settlements were not necessary and often impossible. Wherever possible and justified by supply, a trading post was established, the "port" consisting simply of the ships, anchored some distance offshore and serviced by native-manned surf boats plying between the vessels and the open beach. This helps to explain the relative lack of emphasis placed during this early period upon the coastal lands east of Freetown and along the Gulf of Guinea, where the combined factors of a coast fringed with dangerous sandbars, swamps, and lagoons, the virtual lack of good harbors for port development, and the forbidding tropical rainforest hinterland tended to inhibit trade and human settlement. It was, however, the chief source of slaves for the Americas. This initially limited trade and settlement pattern had virtually no effect upon subsequent port development along this coast.

The western coast of West Africa, on the other hand, with a large submerged ria coastline offering easy shelter, two large rivers (the Senegal and the Gambia) offering fairly easy access to the interior, a relatively favorable climatic hinterland, and its relative closeness to Europe, was early an area of contention among the major powers of Europe. The early and continuous occupancy of the valley of the Gambia River by the English coupled with the eventual control of most of Senegal as it is now by the French conditioned the present-day pattern of port development along this coast. With the use of the Gambia River denied them (despite their trading post at Albreda), the French from the first used the Senegal River as a route to the interior, with Saint Louis as its outlet. There is little doubt that had France managed to secure control of the Gambia River it would have become the principal penetration route into the Sudan, and that somewhere along its course the equivalent to and substitute for Saint Louis (and later Dakar) would have developed. Gorée and its nearby mainland trading station of Rufisque developed early as modest forerunners to the eventual port of Dakar. In any event, with the abolition of the slave trade by the Congress of Vienna in 1815, Europe began to lose most of its economic interest in West Africa, an interest which gradually reappeared with the increased large-scale raw material demands of the industrial revolution.

The second and most important period in the development of the port pattern of West Africa today had its beginnings with that of the development of the great modern industrial states of western and central Europe, a development sustained by the supply of large quantities of raw materials for the expanding industries and foodstuffs required by the ever increasing urban populations as well as the finding of markets for the finished products. It was then that Europe turned once again to Africa, though not the Africa of small isolated coastal trading posts with limited access to the interior, but the now familiar Africa of solid "spheres of influence" and "colonial annexation." West Africa, with its luxurious tropical rainforest and savanna belts in relative close proximity to Europe, was the first attraction. This attraction was enhanced by the natural stands of industrially valuable wild rubber and oil palm plus the possibility of commercial production of cacao, coffee, hemp, cotton, sugar, and peanuts.

The preparatory work for the establishment of spheres of influence in West Africa was performed by the numerous French, British, and German explorers who, from as early as the eighteenth century, penetrated and explored the interior of this vast region. Note has already been made of the early French penetration into the Sudanese interior via the Senegal River for the purpose of widening the traditional trade in gold and gum, an exploration which was the forerunner of the great French consolidation of virtually the entire West African Sudan. This was followed by the British explorations of Houghton, who died in 1791 near Nioro in what is now Mali during his attempt to reach Timbuktu; Mungo Park, who between 1795 and 1797 and in 1805 explored the upper reaches of the Niger River; Clapperton, who crossed the Sahara from Tripoli to Lake Chad in 1823, and who died at Sokoto in 1827; Laing, who in 1825 was the first European to visit Timbuktu; and the

Lander brothers, whose descent of the Niger River from Bussa to the Gulf of Guinea in 1830 laid the foundation for the subsequent British claim to present-day Nigeria. The French, after their reacquisition of Senegal in 1815, were represented by Mollien, who in 1819 traced the sources of the Senegal and Gambia rivers and visited the Fouta Djalon, and Caillié, who in 1827–1828 marched from what is now Guinea to Morocco via the Fouta Djalon, Kankan, Timbuktu, and the Sahara. And finally, one cannot omit mention of the German Dr. Heinrich Barth, who from 1850 to 1855 made the first thorough geographical study of the central Sudan from Lake Chad to Timbuktu. Thus by the middle of the nineteenth century the basis was set for the establishment of European spheres of influence in West Africa, an institution which had a profound effect upon the region's future pattern of port development.

The first drive into the interior in the hope of securing a solid territorial annex to existing coastal stations was made by France under the dynamic leadership of the man who was to become the symbol of French colonialism in West Africa—General Louis Faidherbe, later the governor of Senegal in 1854. Ignoring the advice of Captain Bouët-Willaumez[1] and others who advocated the penetration and conquest of West Africa from the old and weak trading posts in Dahomey and from the newly established stations in the Ivory Coast, Liberia, and Guinea, and succumbing to the traditions of "le Fleuve," Faidherbe continued (but considerably expanded) the policy of using Saint Louis as the French base of operation in West Africa. Beginning with an agreement signed in 1857 with Great Britain, under the terms of which both states agreed to respect each other's respective territorial claims in Senegal and the Gambia, Faidherbe began his double drive: (1) to consolidate French holdings in Senegal, and (2) to push French influence eastward into the upper Senegal and upper and middle Niger river basins. The first goal was achieved with only a moderate success, since it was not until well after the turn of the century that complete and final pacification of Casamance was brought about. The success of the second objective was more immediate. With the defeat of El Hadj Omar, the chief of the Toucouleurs, near Kayes in 1857 and Mage's expedition to Ségou in 1861, the door was opened for French control of the entire middle Niger Valley. Despite a momentary lapse during and immediately following her defeat in the Franco-Prussian War of 1870–1871 and the subsequent restoration of the Republic, France continued to push eastward, a push spurred on by the kindling of British and German expansionist policies in West Africa and the signing in 1885 of the General Act of the International Congress of Berlin calling for "effective occupation" as a prerequisite for the establishment of colonies and protectorates in Africa. In 1899–1900, with the joining in Chad of the three principal columns—Joalland-Meynier from the western Sudan, Gentil from the Congo, and Foureau and Lamy from North Africa via the Sahara—French control of virtually all the western and central Sudanese zone was assured to an inland distance of over 3,000 kilometers behind the Atlantic coastal ports of Saint Louis, Rufisque, and the newly created Dakar.

While the French were expending great efforts in the penetration and colonization of Senegal and the Sudanese interior along the traditional route of the Senegal River, the British were beginning to show signs of a reawakened enthusiasm along the lower coast of West Africa, an enthusiasm unfortunately not immediately shared by the French. Shortly after the Landers' discovery of the true course of the Niger River, British traders were busy operating along its lower reaches. Following the establishment of Lagos as a crown colony in 1861 and the declaration in 1885 of the Oils River Protectorate along the coastal territory from Lagos to the Cameroons, French influence along this favored stretch of the Guinea Coast and along the lower course of the Niger River was permanently excluded. This was confirmed by the Anglo-French treaty of August 5, 1890. Subsequent inland penetration by the Royal Niger Company as far as Lake Chad in the northeast and Sokoto in the northwest brought British claims in direct conflict with those of France, a dispute which was settled by the accord of 1898 delimiting the southern boundary of French rule in eastern West Africa.

A similar early aggressive policy on the part of the British assured them control of the favored Gold Coast (now Ghana). By securing the remaining Danish and Dutch trading posts in 1850 and 1871, respectively, and subsequently creating the Gold Coast Colony in 1874, the British managed to ensure for themselves sole possession of this stretch of the southern coast, the inland extension of which was also defined by the Anglo-French agreement of 1898. The highly favored port of Free-town and the surrounding Sierra Leone Peninsula were declared a crown colony in 1808, the surrounding territorial annexations of which were constituted as the Sierra Leone Protectorate in 1898. Thus early in the scramble for West African colonies and protectorates the British acquired the four choice territories (including the Gambia) of West Africa, choice in that they included the best means of access to the interior, most of the good sites for port development, the densest populations, and/or areas with the brightest economic potential. France, in her preoccupation with Senegal, the Senegal River, and the Sudan, was forced to take second choice along the Guinea Coast.

Failing to follow the advice of Bouët-Willaumez, who advocated the extension of French rule in West Africa from trading posts that he restored or established before the middle of the nineteenth century along the Guinea Coast in present-day Dahomey, the Ivory Coast, Liberia, and Guinea, France belatedly entered the scramble for colonies along this coast. Although French trading posts were restored in Dahomey in 1841, it was not until 1878 and 1883 that Cotonou and Porto-Novo, respectively, were officially annexed by France, and not until the last decade of the century that Portuguese, German, and British claims to the territory were vacated. In 1894 the colony of Dahomey was created, a colony which soon pushed into the interior of West Africa to link up with the main east-west French axis at the Niger River. French claims along the Ivory Coast date from the establishment of trading posts by Bouët-Willaumez in 1843 at Grand-Bassam, Assinie, and Dabou. Nothing further was done to extend French claims far into the interior until 1889 when, out of fear of British linkage of the Gold Coast with Sierra Leone and the possible consequent cutting of the Ivory Coast's potential land bond with French Sudan, the explorer Binger, coming from Bamako, joined up with the columns of the trader Treich-Laplène coming from the coast. Four years later, the Ivory Coast Colony was proclaimed.

Similarly, French expansionist policies in French Guinea were conditioned to a very large extent by British policies in West Africa, and not as the result of long-range positive planning. From the nucleus trading post founded in 1849 at Boké, French penetration and occupation of present-day Guinea was encouraged as a countermeasure to British pressure in joining Sierra Leone with the Gambia. Following the elimination of German interests in 1885 and the signing of boundary accords with the British and Portuguese in 1882 and 1886, respectively, Guinea became a French colony in 1891. Thus by the end of the nineteenth century France was assured three outlets along the Gulf of Guinea—three territories contiguous with the main body of French penetration of West Africa but lacking in natural routes to the interior and without favorable sites for port development. This was the price paid by France for her preoccupation with Senegal and her dreams of imperialism on a continental scale. With the creation in 1895 of the Government-General of French West Africa under a civilian authority and the attachment to it of Dahomey in 1899, Niger in 1911, and Mauritania in 1920, the historical and political basis for the pattern and development of the maritime port system in the federation was clearly defined.

The birth of Mauritania in 1904 completed the political map of West Africa, and brought to a close the scramble for colonies. In addition to the eventual eight colonies (subsequently territories) of French West Africa (Senegal, Mauritania, French Sudan, French Guinea, the Ivory Coast, Upper Volta, Niger, and Dahomey) and the four colonial enclaves of British West Africa (the Gambia, Sierra Leone, the Gold Coast, and Nigeria), Germany and Portugal managed to retain single footholds in the region: Togoland and Portuguese Guinea. Independent Liberia completed the picture, managing to survive the period of colonial expansion intact. Subsequent modification, prior to the political changes initiated by Ghana's independence in 1957, was limited to the removal of Germany from the scene after her defeat in World War I and the creation of the double French and British mandates (subsequently trusteeships) over Togoland in her stead. It should be noted that the creation of a French mandate over eastern Togoland (French Togo) did not mean the economic or political inclusion of this territory within French West Africa as is often assumed, but led to its separate development. British Togo, also administered separately from the Gold Coast, was absorbed by Ghana with the coming of independence. Today West Africa consists of fourteen independent states (including the eight states of former French West Africa), and the Portuguese overseas province of Guinea, or, more

TABLE 7   Areas and Populations of the Political Units of West Africa
(*Estimated as of January 1, 1964*)

Countries	Area in Square Kilometers	Area in Square Miles	Population
West African Community			
Senegal	197,161	76,124	3,300,000
Mauritania	1,085,806	419,230	800,000
Mali	1,204,024	464,874	4,450,000
Ivory Coast	322,463	124,503	3,500,000
Upper Volta	274,201	105,869	4,600,000
Niger	1,188,797	458,995	3,250,000
Dahomey	115,763	44,696	2,200,000
Other Countries			
Gambia	10,381	4,008	320,000
Sierra Leone	72,326	27,925	2,600,000
Ghana	237,873	91,843	7,450,000
Nigeria	923,773	356,669	37,600,000
Liberia	111,370	43,000	1,360,000
Guinea	245,856	94,925	3,300,000
Togo	56,592	21,850	1,580,000
Port. Guinea	36,125	13,948	555,000
Total	6,082,511	2,348,459	76,865,000
Total area and population of Senegal, Mauritania, and Mali	2,486,991	960,228	8,550,000
% of total area of Senegal, Mauritania, and Mali to the total area of West Africa			40.89
% of total population of Senegal, Mauritania, and Mali to the total population of West Africa			11.12

Source: Modified from Edward B. Espenshade, Jr. (ed.), *Goode's World Atlas* (12th ed.; Chicago: Rand McNally & Company, 1964), p. 170.

popularly, Portuguese Guinea, in reality a Portuguese colony (see Table 7 and Fig. 1).

The existing maritime port and connecting hinterland communications pattern of West Africa has been considerably influenced and conditioned by the historical development of the region. Political jealousies, strategic considerations, and parochial economic attitudes dictated that commercial intercourse and lines of communication not cross, wherever possible, the boundaries of the respective spheres of influence. This attitude was particularly true of the French who, as was noted, gained dominion over the vast bulk of the West African hinterland whose closest and/or most economical coastal outlets often were in British or Liberian territory. In Dahomey the coastal terminus of the never fully completed Benin-Niger Railroad and the connecting roads into Niger and eastern Upper Volta was the wharf at Cotonou, irrespective of the fact that the far superior port of Lagos, in British Nigeria, was located only 120 kilometers to the east. Similarly, the Mossi country of Upper Volta was connected to the coast by the arc-shaped Abidjan-Niger Railroad to the port of Abidjan in the Ivory Coast, and not with the more direct ocean outlets in the Gold Coast. A similar situation developed in French Guinea, where the Conakry-Niger Railroad was constructed to drain the remote Guinea Highlands through the port of Conakry, a distance almost twice as long as an equivalent outlet in Liberia would have been. And finally, the fourth (and perhaps the most important) railroad in former French West Africa was the Dakar-Niger line, whose main trunk was extended from the port of Dakar to the heart of the Sudanese interior at Bamako and Koulikoro on the Niger River in French Sudan.

While a large portion of this interior hinterland could easily have been drained by ports along the Gulf of Guinea (as indeed it has been during the recent crisis between Senegal and Mali), factors of historical impetus, location, and coastal geography, as well as political considerations dictated that the principal flow of goods from this area to the coast and the reciprocal inflow of imports move along an east-west axis (see Chapter 5). With severe limitations imposed on the use of the Senegal River and the port of Saint Louis as the main transportation axis and port, economic expediency soon dictated the need for a better transportation link and port. Unfortunately, the historical development of West Africa, coupled with the aforementioned determination of the French to keep their territorial lines of communication under their flag, precluded the use of the natural outlet for the West African Sudan—the British-controlled Gambia River. The full use of this river as the principal artery of trade would have enabled deep-draft vessels to penetrate easily a distance of 240 kilometers into the Sudan, enabled shallow-draft vessels to reach 470 kilometers inland throughout the course of a year, and obviated at least the last 100 kilometers of the existing rail haul to Dakar. As an alternative the French developed the port of Dakar and the Dakar-Niger Railroad.[2]

Historical Development of the Port of Dakar

Although definite French implantation in Senegal dates from the establishment of Bieurt near the mouth of the Senegal River in 1638, the historical development of the port of Dakar proper can be traced only from 1857. Prior to this date the French colony of Senegal consisted of a permanent settlement at Saint Louis and several temporary, poorly staffed trading stations along the Senegal River, at Gorée, along the "Petite-Côte," [3] and in Casamance. The mainland in general (and Cape Verde Peninsula in particular) was unattractive for permanent settlement owing to the difficulties of the natural environment (the absence of building materials, the absence of permanent sources of water, and/or poor soils for agriculture) and the problem of frequent native attacks. It should be noted, however, that despite the apparent lack of enthusiasm on the part of the French to settle the mainland, most of Cape Verde Peninsula (including the site of modern Dakar) was officially ceded to the French by the Damel (King) of Cayor in a series of treaties executed in 1764, 1765, and 1787.[4]

The first major attempt, albeit not an official one, at colonizing Cape Verde Peninsula and the establishment of a permanent European community was undertaken in 1817 by the Société Coloniale Philanthropique, a successor to the Société Coloniale Africaine. This privately financed venture had as its goal the establishment of European agricultural communities on the peninsula. On April 12, 1817, the sailing vessel *Belle Alexandrine* arrived at Gorée from Le Havre with 175 hopeful settlers. Unfortunately, within two months the venture was abandoned as a complete failure. The almost total lack of wood for fuel and building purposes, the lack of surface water or springs, the excessively sandy soil, and the scorching climate had taken their toll. No subsequent serious efforts were made to claim Cape Verde Peninsula effectively for France or to establish permanent European settlments on the Peninsula until 1857, although note should be made of the Roman Catholic mission established in 1847 on the site of present-day Dakar by the Mission des Pères du Saint-Esprit, of a few scattered farms belonging to residents of Gorée, and of occasional temporary trading posts established by Gorée traders along the shores of Dakar Bay.

In 1849 Captain (later Colonel) J. M. E. Pinet-Laprade of the French Army Corps of Engineers (Corps du Génie), whose name was later to rank among the great colonial figures of France, was assigned to Saint Louis. Six years later, in February 1855, he was reassigned to Gorée as military commander, and almost immediately turned his attention to the development of the mainland. He wrote:

We can almost certainly conclude that the establishment of a railroad between [Saint Louis] and Dakar will be possible in a few years. It will produce a revolution in the commercial activities of Senegal, and at the same time promote the development of our establishments on Cape Verde Peninsula.[5]

In a similar though less encouraging vein, the following unsigned article appeared in the official publication of the colonial government of Senegal, *Le Moniteur du Sénégal,* on June 17, 1856:

We recognize . . . that Dakar has a future, and ought to become more important than it is, but its development must depend exclusively upon the growth of agricultural production in Cayor and Baol. It does not appear to us that Dakar has the potential of ever becoming the principal port of Senegal. Here are the reasons why.

Most important is the fact that the roadstead of Dakar is not well delimited and not very deep, and ships, in order to be out of danger there, must remain a great distance offshore.

The larger ships would take at least 30 days to debark and embark at Dakar, while 10 days would be sufficient at Saint Louis, where they could anchor in the river alongside the quay.

Furthermore, the operating costs on a beach such as at Dakar would be considerably more because the ships would have to remain anchored very far from the point of ultimate debarkation.

Not only would the merchants [of Saint Louis] be deprived of the advantage of having all the transactions take place under their scrutiny, but they would have to maintain an agent at Dakar and also have large warehouses for storing the goods coming from Europe and from Saint Louis. Certain goods depreciate in value by frequent handlings. Goods with a large volume and little value, such as peanuts, would find it very difficult to afford the cost of transportation from the railroad station at Saint Louis to Dakar, be put into warehouses at Dakar, and then be placed aboard ships.

One could expand on this list of inconveniences that would result in shifting the main port of Senegal from Saint Louis to Dakar, but it is best to say that the difficulties of the sandbar [at Saint Louis] will be surmounted by the use of a dredge when one seriously wishes it to be done.

Dakar cannot, therefore, according to us, become the principal port of Senegal.[6]

Nevertheless, on January 29, 1857, Admiral Hamelin, French Minister of the Navy and of the Colonies, acting largely on the advice of Pinet-Laprade, authorized the establishment of two forts and a permanent town at the site of what was to become Dakar. On May 25, 1857, Captain A. L. Protet of the frigate *Jeanne d'Arc,* acting on the orders of Admiral Hamelin, landed a detachment of sailors at the site, and officially laid claim to Cape Verde Peninsula for France. Four months later the first permanent and continuous settlement at Dakar was established.

The port of Dakar proper had its indirect beginning on June 17, 1857, when the French government established a new postal route between Bordeaux and the La Plata Estuary in South America. Three months later an agreement was signed between the government and a private steamship company, the Compagnie des Messageries Impériales, calling for the establishment of a regular fifteen-day departure service between France and South America, the steamships leaving from Bordeaux and Marseilles and touching at Lisbon and Gorée. The inadequacy of the small harbor at Gorée for the creation of a large-scale coaling station was almost immediately recognized. Consequently, in November 1858, a small, though still inadequate, wharf was completed in Dakar Bay by the steamship company at the site of present-day Pier II, behind which a coal storage yard was constructed. The coal was transferred to the ships anchored in the open of Dakar Bay by means of lighters. This wharf was also used by the military for the debarkation of supplies used to consolidate their newly declared rights on the mainland. In addition, a request was made for a change in the charter of the company to enable it to substitute Saint Vincent in the Portuguese colony of Cape Verde Islands for Gorée on the Bordeaux–South America run. The Marseilles–South America service was to continue calling at Gorée and Dakar for partial bunkering and at Santa Cruz de Tenerife in the Canary Islands, a Spanish colony, for the remainder. The request was approved effective February 21, 1861, subject to a retransfer to Senegal upon the completion of an adequate bunkering port in the vicinity of Dakar.

The need for a larger port, preferably on the mainland, to enable the French colony to compete effectively for the Atlantic bunkering trade with the older and more favorably located Portuguese and Spanish insular ports was generally agreed upon; the only open question was the one of location. On November 5, 1859, the Minister for Algeria and the Colonies instructed the governor of Senegal to name a board of study to investigate the matter and to select a site for the new port. On January 15, 1860, the nine-man committee issued its report. After visiting Saint Vincent and various possible sites on and near Cape Verde Peninsula, three possible locations were finally selected: (1) Gorée Island, then the administrative and commercial capital of southern Senegal; (2) Bernard Bay, at the southern end of Cape Verde Peninsula near Cape Manuel; and (3) Dakar Bay, the site of the first installations of the Compagnie des Messageries Impériales (see Fig. 9). The first was rejected because of its small harbor and insularity; the second because of the restrictions imposed by the basaltic cliffs behind the bay plus the necessity of constructing a deep, costly protective jetty. Dakar Bay was finally selected because it offered fairly good natural protection, possessed sufficient level land behind the bay for port and commercial development, and offered easy potential contact with the main body of Senegal to the east. Thus the first formative plans for the eventual modern port of Dakar were well under way.

Work on the port was started in February 1862. The recently completed lighterage wharf was extended and converted into a 300-meter solid jetty, thus offering greater protection near the shore to the lighters operating between the ships anchored in the open bay and the wharf. But even before this project was finished, Colonel Pinet-Laprade began to champion the construction of an even larger jetty behind which the ships themselves could anchor and undertake loading and unloading operations in calm water. In 1864 the construction of this jetty, rooted on Dakar Point and extending a distance of 330 meters in the direction of Bel-Air Point, was undertaken. This was the beginning of what is now South

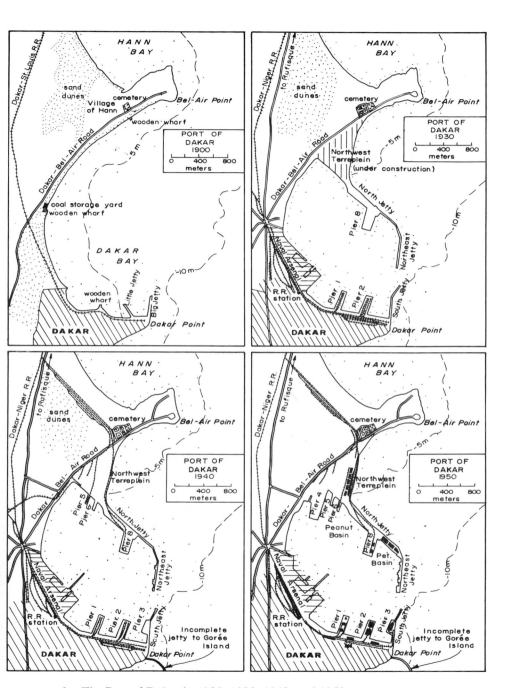

FIG. 9   The Port of Dakar in 1900, 1930, 1940, and 1950

Jetty. With the erection that same year of a lighthouse at the Mamelles, followed two years later by the construction of lighthouses at Almadi Point and Cape Manuel, full protection from the treacherous rocky coast was afforded ships approaching the port. On November 4, 1866, work on the new port and its approaches was completed, and the Compagnie des Messageries Impériales switched its full operations back to Dakar. The pattern of today's port of Dakar was beginning to take recognizable form. It should be noted, however, that with the exception of a few minor trading posts Dakar was a town without any importance outside the bunkering sphere; its population consisted almost entirely of port workers.

Thirty static years followed. Despite the completion of the Dakar-Saint Louis Railroad in 1885, Dakar remained principally a coaling station until shortly after the turn of the century. Rufisque, settled in 1861 and also on the Dakar-Saint Louis rail line, became the important commercial peanut center of Senegal. Gorée lost its commercial importance in the last quarter of the nineteenth century partly to Dakar but mainly to Rufisque. Despite its inferior natural site and facilities, Rufisque became the leading "port" of Senegal, consisting simply of an unprotected open wharf protruding into open Gorée Bay. It drew virtually the entire commercial peanut crop of the colony and attracted a large inflow of investment capital. While Rufisque prospered, the far superior port of Dakar, only 25 kilometers away and the terminus of the rail line passing through Rufisque, consisted of a "hideous mass of huts, warehouses, and mediocre official buildings." [7] Within a relatively short period of time, however, a complete reversal was to take place, with Dakar assuming the dominant role in Senegalese economic and political affairs, and Rufisque being relegated to the status of a secondary, unkempt, provincial town.

The full outlines of the modern port of Dakar had their beginnings in 1898, when it was decided to convert the port into an up-to-date naval base by the prolongation of South Jetty to its present length of 500 meters, the construction of North Jetty to its present length of 2,080 meters, and the construction of the naval base on the flat, sandy stretch to the west of the harbor. Within these limits, a body of water over 250 hectares (approximately one square mile) in surface area was to be confined. In 1908 work was completed, and the finest naval base between Gibraltar and the Cape of Good Hope was put into operation. But hardly had this work been undertaken when the Chamber of Commerce of Gorée, acting on behalf of Dakar, called for the simultaneous construction of a large, modern port of commerce within the larger confines. Despite the expected opposition to the proposal from Rufisque, which claimed to be an adequate drainer of the Senegalese peanut crop, and Saint Louis, which claimed priority for itself in port development, the proposal was accepted in 1903. Work was started in 1904, and the new commercial port was completed in 1910. In addition to the two outer protective jetties and the naval base, the port then consisted of two 300-meter piers on the south side of the harbor bordered by accostable quays and backed by open storage space.

Within three years, however, even these facilities proved to be inadequate for the rapidly expanding economy of Senegal, and money was appropriated for port expansion. Following the war-induced delay, work was started in 1926 on the development of the North Zone of the port, until then consisting solely of an unused protective jetty. With the completion in 1933 of the bunkering and peanut zones to the north and the construction soon thereafter of Pier III in the South Zone, the existing pattern of the port of Dakar was set by the outbreak of World War II. Subsequent modifications varied the form of the port but not its substance. Finally, note should be made of the last major attempt at port modification: an attempt to connect Gorée Island with the mainland by means of a jetty, and thus to protect the outer harbor from the seasonal southern gales. This project, started in 1938, was interrupted in 1943 owing to the scarcity of supplies and credit, and was never completed. Had it been completed, the harbor of Dakar would unquestionably have ranked among the world's finest—a designation nevertheless that it probably still deserves.

3 / Port Facilities
and Traffic

THE SECOND requirement of a port in addition to shelter is that of sufficiently ample facilities to satisfy its essential functions. That these facilities are generally more than ample in the case of the port of Dakar is indicated by the fact that in normal years the port is used to approximately one-third of maximum capacity with no period of the year approaching 100 per cent.[1] However, certain shortcomings in the event of an emergency made their appearance during the Suez Canal crisis of 1956–1957, when Suez shipping was necessarily rerouted around the Cape of Good Hope. During this period (August 1956 to June 1957), a total of 1,446 ships which normally would have passed through the Canal called at Dakar for bunker provisions. The peak was reached in March 1957, when a total of 258 rerouted vessels called at Dakar, representing 40 per cent of the total port entries for the month (see Fig. 10). During this crisis, two important deficiencies were noted: (1) the insufficient total storage capacity (191,354 cubic meters) of the Petroleum Zone to meet emergency requirements[2] and (2) the inability of the port to accommodate modern deep-draft supertankers because their maximum drafts exceed the maximum permissible 11-meter draft of the harbor. Since the future calls for the greater use of such tankers and freighters, consideration will have to be given to increasing the depth of the inner harbor by additional dredging. The construction of the new petroleum refinery with its floating tanker terminal just north of the port has already partially ameliorated this difficulty as well as the problem of emergency petroleum storage facilities (see Chapter 4). In any event, it should be emphasized that the facilities of the port are today generally more than adequate to satisfy most normal demands placed upon it.

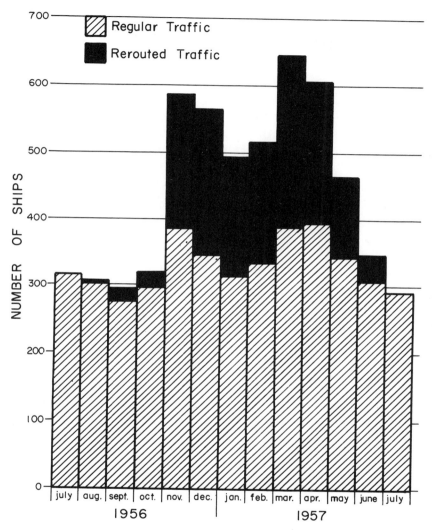

FIG. 10   Regular and rerouted traffic calling at the Port of Dakar during the Suez Canal crisis of 1956–1957

With the completion of the new fishing quay and the most recent dredging operations early in 1964, the interior harbor of the port has an exposed area of 210 hectares (519 acres), of which 89 hectares (220 acres) are open to ships having maximum drafts of between 10 and 11 meters. Other comparable figures are: 93 hectares (230 acres) dredged to a depth of −5 to −9 meters and 28 hectares (69 acres) not yet dredged. The funds for these dredging operations (as well as for the construction of the new fishing facilities) were provided by the European Development Fund of the European Economic Community. The natural and man-made barriers of the port provide the harbor with excellent shelter from winds and swells, which only occasionally interfere with ship movements during the rainy season which lasts from late June until the beginning of November. With a mean tidal range of only 1.15 meters (spring tidal range of 1.90 meters; neap tidal range of 0.40 meters) and natural currents preventing sedimentation, periodic dredging of the rocky bottom to keep the channels open is not necessary. These factors coupled with generally favorable approaches (except for the rocky immediate vicinity of the peninsula) make the harbor of Dakar one of the finest in Africa.

At the completion of the port improvement projects of the First Four Year Plan (1961 to 1964 inclusive), the port of Dakar (exclusive of the Naval Arsenal) contained 46 berths and 8,466 meters of alongside quays consisting of the following stretches of alongside depths: 5,461 meters usable to a depth of −8 to −12 meters; 1,600 meters usable to a depth of —4 to —7.2 meters; and 1,405 meters usable to a depth of 0 to —3 meters. In addition, the designated commercial port area consists of approximately 682,000 square meters of level land (of which 57,000 square meters contain closed warehouses) and contains 21 kilometers of standard meter-gauge railroad track connected to the main line of the Régie des Chemins de Fer du Sénégal (the Senegal Railroad). There are petroleum-bunkering storage tanks (capacity of 191,354 cubic meters) in the Northeast Zone of the port, with additional storage facilities in nearby Bel-Air and Park A and at the new refinery.

The commercial port is divided into four zones, each of which serves a distinct function: the South, West, Northwest, and Northeast zones. The oldest of these is the South Zone, immediately adjacent to the old

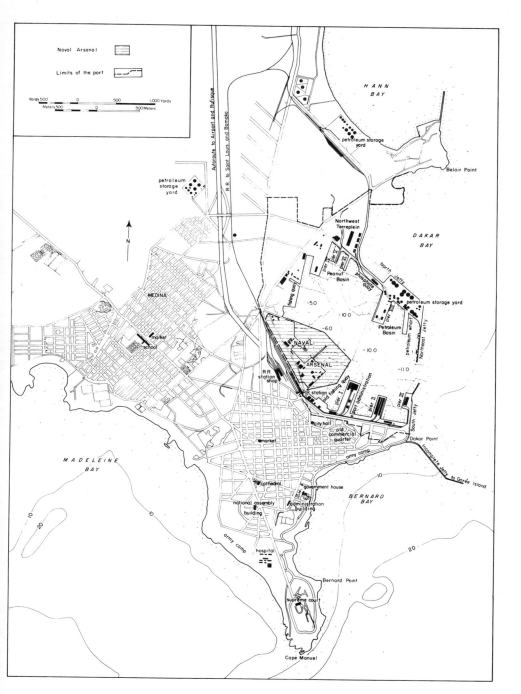

FIG. 11   The City and Port of Dakar

FIG. 12   Aerial view of the Port of Dakar
Credit: Photo Aérienne, Verbelke

FIG. 13   Aerial view of the South Zone of the Port of Dakar and the City
of Dakar
Credit: Photo Aérienne, Verbelke

FIG. 14   Pier III: The Mali Free Trade Port in the South Zone of the Port of Dakar

commercial quarter of the city of Dakar. This zone was the site of the original port installations at Dakar and, except for the two berths reserved for fishing vessels, is today generally reserved for the manipulation of general cargo. This zone consists of three piers numbered I, II, and III and adjacent quay space, with a total of 22 deep-water berths. In 1963, when agreement was reached between Senegal and Mali to reopen the railroad between the two states, it was also agreed to turn Pier III into a free port area for the transit of goods to and from Mali. This scheme has been put into effect, and today the activities of this free port area are in the hands of Malian authorities and are separate and distinct from those of the remainder of the commercial port. However, port statistics do include the activities at this pier. The South Zone also contains 12 general warehouses with a total covered area of 30,080 square meters, a cold-storage warehouse with a refrigerated capacity of 10,000 cubic meters, and 11 traveling gantry cranes, the seven largest of which have a capacity of 6 tons and a vertical lift of 27 meters. Highly capable local crews man these permanent and additional mobile facilities as well as the loading and unloading facilities aboard the vessels. This zone, as well as the entire commercial port, is efficiently and neatly run, and is considered to be perhaps the most efficient of the West African Community.[3] The port of Abidjan, running at virtual maximum capacity and in a state of flux, has yet to settle down to such an orderly execution of duties. In general, the facilities of the South Zone have been more than adequate to satisfy all general cargo demands, and no present plans exist for its expansion. The only serious problem of this zone is one dealing with the Mali free port area. Owing to the inconvertibility of the Malian franc,[4] Mali has had difficulty in meeting her payments to Senegal for the use of the port area and the Senegal Railroad. At one time, the possibility existed that the use of these facilities would have to be denied to Mali. During the late summer of 1964, however, the two states agreed

FIG. 15 Moving general cargo at Pier I, South Zone

that Mali would reduce her deficit by increasing her exports to Senegal. It is very possible that Mali will face continued difficulties in complying with the terms of this agreement owing to the very limited resource base of the country and the similar nature of the general economies of the two countries. In this eventuality, the importance of developing Mali's embryonic ties with the port of Abidjan in the Ivory Coast becomes evident. The complementary nature of the economies of Mali and the Ivory Coast should preclude similar difficulties between these two countries.

Moving clockwise around the inner harbor, one comes next to the West Zone, which extends for approximately two and one-half kilometers along the western shore between Pier I and Pier IV and includes the Naval Arsenal. Bordered largely by gently sloping sand deposits which extend into the harbor proper and thus giving rise to naturally shallow harbor depths, this zone is the least developed of the inner harbor and contains virtually the only sites available for large-scale future port de-

FIG. 16   The *S. S. Ouolof,* which provides scheduled passenger and cargo service between Dakar and Ziguinchor

velopment. It is here that the new fishing port has been constructed under the First Four Year Plan, a port completed with funds supplied, as for the dredging operations, by the European Economic Community. Whereas the fishing quay and the cold-storage warehouse of the South Zone are reserved for the unloading, storage, and freezing of fresh fish, the new facilities will be used almost exclusively for the processing and canning of tuna for local and world markets (see Chapter 4). The Naval Arsenal is still the headquarters for the French South Atlantic Fleet and has a dry dock capable of receiving large naval and private vessels having maximum lengths of 187 meters, widths of 25 meters, and drafts of 9 meters. The West Zone also contains three private maritime servicing companies: Manutention Africaine, the Ateliers et Chantiers de Dakar, and the Chantiers Navals de Nianing, with respective slipways of 1,000-ton, 300-ton, and 250-ton capacities. In addition, the Port de Commerce de Dakar and the Entreprise des Travaux du Port maintain repair facilities in this zone for their numerous servicing craft, with respective slipway capacities of 100 and 1,000 tons.

Continuing clockwise around the inner harbor, one comes to the North Jetty, which was converted into the North Zone of the port between 1926 and 1933 (see Chapter 2). This zone is used today almost exclusively for the manipulation of bulk cargo, and contributes heavily to the volume of exports of the port and to virtually all the bunkering activities at Dakar. It is further subdivided into the Northwest Zone (or Peanut Basin) and the Northeast Zone (or Petroleum Basin). The former consists of piers IV, V, and VI, the Société Sénégalaise des Phosphates de Thiès phosphate quay, and the large triangular Northwest Terreplain to the rear. This 11-berth subzone also has witnessed one of the most recent additions to the port of Dakar: the 70,000-ton capacity phosphate storage warehouse built on the Northwest Terreplain and the connecting facilities to and on Pier V for the export of phosphate ore mined by the Compagnie Sénégalaise des Phosphates de Taïba. In addition to Pier V, which is used exclusively for mineral exports, Pier IV serves as the pier for the bulk export of peanuts and peanut cake and as the pier for the bulk importation of grains such as millet, wheat, corn, and rice. The small Pier VI is used chiefly for the import of bulk wine and for the loading of the return cargo of peanut oil. The Société Sénégalaise des Phosphates de Thiès, a subsidiary of the famous European concern of Péchiney-Saint-Gobain, maintains a 35,000-ton-capacity phosphate-storage warehouse and quay for the loading of the mineral between piers VI and VIII. The 250,000-square-meter Northwest Terreplain, constructed originally for the storage of peanuts prior to shipment but which, with the large increase in African oil processing following the close of World War II, has seen its bulk storage use dwindle, has now been encroached upon by the new phosphate warehouse, the Lesieur peanut-oil plant, four peanut-oil and four wine-storage tanks, and the storage facilities of the Compagnie des Pétroles Total d'Afrique de l'Ouest (COPETAO).

The Northeast Zone rounds out the port of Dakar. It includes Pier VIII, formerly solely a coal bunkering pier but now used largely by those ships wishing to take on oil and water while performing commercial activities, the very modern Petroleum Wharf, and the Northeast Jetty, which also contains two bunkering berths. Backing up these piers is the petroleum-storage yard, where subsidiaries of five large international oil companies (Mory, Esso, Shell, British Petroleum, and Mobil Oil) have a combined storage capacity of 191,354 cubic meters. With its thirteen berths (one of which can service only small fishing vessels), efficient labor force, and easy access, the Petroleum Basin has enabled the port of Dakar to compete successfully with the slightly lower-cost competitors of Las Palmas and Santa Cruz de Tenerife in the Canary Islands, the factor of quicker turnabout in this period of high operating costs providing the incentive to use Dakar.

Thus the facilities and equipment of the port of Dakar have been arranged so as to cope with the different types of traffic arriving at the port and to maximize the efficiency of its distribution. This factor coupled with a relatively stable and dependable labor force (there have been no labor difficulties since the proclamation of Senegalese independence in 1960) and a progressive public port management enables the port to offer quick commercial and bunkering operations. The natural factors of site and location have been taken advantage of and improved upon by man to produce one of the finest and busiest ports in tropical Africa. Since it is operating at one-third capacity and with no bottlenecks in its normal operations, there will very likely be no substantial changes in the basic structure of the port in the immediate future.

Nature of the Shipping Calling at the Port

The importance of Dakar as a bunkering port is shown in a study prepared late in 1966 by the port authorities.[5] It shows that in 1965 approximately 84 per cent of the 4,256 ships calling at the port came for the sole or partial purpose of taking on provisions:

40.79 per cent called solely for provisions;

43.12 per cent called partially for provisions and partially for commercial operations;

9.14 per cent called solely for commercial operations; and

6.95 per cent called neither for commercial operations nor for provisions.[6]

A ratio of between 70 and 80 per cent calling for provisions is considered normal, and the bunkering facilities of the port are so geared.[7] Only during exceptional periods, such as the Suez Canal crisis when both this percentage and the total number of ships calling at Dakar suddenly increased, are bunkering facilities sometimes strained, causing occasional delays. The slightly higher percentage for 1965 is probably an anomaly. However, future statistics will indicate if the 70 to 80 per cent ratio will have to be modified in future port planning.

As is true for most colonial and ex-colonial territories, the ships of the former metropolitan power calling at the port of Dakar rank high in terms of the percentage calling at the port, although in Dakar French ships entering the port account for considerably less than 50 per cent of the total number. This relatively low percentage is explained by the nature of the port (an important international port of call and bunkering center) and by the fact that in the post-independence period many ships which formerly flew the French flag are now under African registration. Although no official preference is accorded to ships of French registry (except that those working in regular liner service—mainly French—are given berthing priority), ships flying the French tricolor accounted for 29 per cent of the total number and 31 per cent of the net registered tonnage of the ships calling at the port in 1965 (see Tables 8, 9, and 10).

Over twenty shipping lines provide regular and frequent cargo service between Dakar and the principal ports of Europe, North America, South

TABLE 8   Comparative Movement of Ships, Goods, and Passengers at the Port of Dakar for 1938, 1948, 1958, 1964, and 1965

	1938	1948	1958	1964	1965
Ship movements					
Ships entered					
Number	3,427	2,099*	4,117	4,231	4,256
Total net registered					
tonnage (1,000 tons)	7,359	4,423*	10,071	11,535	11,805
Ships left					
Number	3,433	2,099*	4,067	4,222	4,262
Total net registered					
tonnage (1,000 tons)	7,368	4,423*	10,047	11,512	11,813
Goods movements (1,000 tons)					
Debarkations	1,241	1,218	2,213	1,913	1,783
Petroleum products	746	468	1,513	1,006	1,873
Other cargo	495	750	700	908	910
Embarkations	1,150	797	1,673	2,314	2,357
Bunker provisions					
(excluding water)	723	332	1,071	917	880
Cargo	427	465	602	1,397	1,477
Passenger movements					
Debarked	12,236	20,312	28,155	22,436	19,178
Embarked	10,481	15,729	34,379	34,462	23,706
In transit	n.a.	n.a.	73,375	25,034	22,416

* Figures are approximate.

n.a.—Figures are not available.

Sources: (a) Port de Commerce de Dakar, *Renseignements Statistiques Comparés, 1957* (Rufisque: Imprimerie du Haut Commissariat, 1958), pp. 14, 27, 56, and 59; (b) République du Sénégal, Ministère des Transports et des Télécommunications, Port de Commerce, *Statistiques Annuelles, 1961*, p. 5; (c) Port Autonome de Dakar, Service des Statistiques, *Statistiques Comparées: Mois de Décembre 1965*, p. 2; and (d) Interpolations by the writer.

America, Asia, and Africa exclusive of the West African coast (see Table 11). Two of these lines, the Nouvelle Compagnie de Paquebots (NCP) and the Compagnie de Navigation Paquet, also provide regular passenger service between France (Bordeaux and Marseilles) and Dakar by means of passenger-cargo liners. In addition, the port is served by numerous unscheduled (tramp) vessels. In 1965 this extra-West African trade accounted for 96 per cent of the total recorded cargo handlings at the port.[8] Owing to the post-independence decrease in intra-West African trade passing through Dakar, it is very unlikely that the percentage role

TABLE 9   Analysis of Ship Movements at the Port of Dakar
by National Registry for 1965

National Registry	% of Total Number Entered	% of Total Net Registered Tonnage Entered
France	28.57	30.62
East Germany	10.67	6.66
United Kingdom	9.89	15.47
Soviet Union	6.63	2.93
Liberia	5.36	7.75
West Germany	4.68	2.63
Norway	4.53	5.78
Italy	4.06	4.83
Netherlands	4.06	2.24
Panama	2.87	3.11
Greece	2.61	2.99
Spain	2.42	1.31
Ghana	1.72	1.77
Sweden	1.55	1.58
Japan	1.34	0.44
Poland	1.20	0.75
Yugoslavia	1.17	1.34
Ivory Coast	1.15	1.11
Denmark	1.10	1.09
United States	0.68	1.27
Switzerland	0.63	0.79
Senegal	0.54	0.33
Nigeria	0.38	0.48
Lebanon	0.38	0.46
Israel	0.38	0.32
Turkey	0.14	0.21
Belgium	0.14	0.20
Morocco	0.14	0.10
Finland	0.12	0.05
Rumania	0.09	0.07
Honduras	0.09	0.04
United Arab Republic	0.09	0.04
Philippines	0.07	0.12
Uruguay	0.07	0.11
Malagasy	0.07	0.08
South Korea	0.07	0.05
Brazil	0.05	0.06
Niger	0.05	0.05

TABLE 9   (*Continued*)

National Registry	% of Total Number Entered	% of Total Net Registered Tonnage Entered
Bulgaria	0.05	0.02
Iceland	0.05	—
Argentina	0.02	0.05
China	0.02	0.04
Somalia	0.02	0.04
Cuba	0.02	0.03
Hungary	0.02	0.01
Gambia	0.02	—
	100.00	100.00

Total number entered	4,256	
Total net registered tonnage entered		11,805,416

Source: Port Autonome de Dakar, Service des Statistiques, *Statistiques Comparées: Mois de Décembre 1965*, pp. 7, 8, 11, and 12.

TABLE 10   Analysis of Ships Entering the Port of Dakar by Types for 1965

Type of Ship	Number	% of Total	Net Registered Tonnage	% of Total
Freighters	2,998	70.44	8,035,044	68.06
Petroleum tankers	211	4.96	1,702,983	14.43
Butane tankers	3	0.07	3,635	0.03
Other tankers	196	4.61	195,545	1.66
Fishing boats	311	7.31	184,034	1.56
Banana boats	188	4.42	466,258	3.95
Ocean liners	130	3.05	854,231	7.24
Refrigerator ships	117	2.75	55,367	0.47
Ore carriers	70	1.64	297,348	2.52
Other ships	32	0.75	10,971	0.09
Total	4,256	100.00	11,805,416	100.00
French	1,216	28.57	3,615,011	30.62
Other	3,040	71.43	8,190,405	69.38

Source: Port Autonome de Dakar, Service des Statistiques, *Statistiques Comparées: Mois de Décembre 1965*, pp. 4 and 6.

TABLE 11   Principal Scheduled Shipping Lines Serving the Port of Dakar and Their Connecting Ports

Shipping Line	*Connecting Ports*
French	
1. Compagnie des Messageries Maritimes	East/South Africa—*Dakar*—Bordeaux—Le Havre—Dunkirk—Antwerp
2. Compagnie Maritime des Chargeurs Réunis	Hamburg—Rotterdam—Amsterdam—Antwerp—Dunkirk—Le Havre—Rouen—Bordeaux—*Dakar*—Conakry—Sassandra—Abidjan—Lomé—Cotonou—Lagos—Douala—Kribi—Libreville—Port Gentil—Pointe Noire
	New York and U.S. east coast ports—*Dakar*—Conakry—Freetown—Monrovia—Abidjan—Takoradi—Tema—Lomé—Cotonou—Lagos—Port Harcourt—Douala—Libreville—Port Gentil—Pointe Noire
	Japan and Hong Kong—Libreville—Douala—Port Harcourt—Lagos—Cotonou—Lomé—Takoradi—Abidjan—Conakry—*Dakar*
3. Compagnie de Navigation Fraissinet et Cyprien Fabre	Marseilles—Palma—North African ports—*Dakar*—Conakry—Monrovia—Sassandra—Abidjan—Takoradi—Lomé—Cotonou—Lagos—Douala—Libreville
4. Compagnie de Navigation Paquet	Marseilles—Tangier—Casablanca—Santa Cruz de Tenerife—*Dakar*
5. Société Navale Delmas-Vieljeux	European ports—West African ports (Port Étienne to Pointe Noire including *Dakar*)
6. Société Navale de l'Ouest	Dunkirk—Le Havre—Bordeaux—*Dakar*—Conakry—Tabou—Abidjan—Lomé—Cotonou—Lagos—Douala—Libreville—Port Gentil—Pointe Noire
7. Nouvelle Compagnie de Paquebots	Bordeaux—Marseilles—Palma—North African ports—*Dakar*—Conakry—Monrovia—Abidjan—Tema—Lomé—Cotonou—Lagos—Douala—Libreville—Pointe Noire

TABLE 11   (*Continued*)

Shipping Line	Connecting Ports
British 8. Palm Line Ltd.	U.K./European/Mediterranean ports and West African ports (including *Dakar*)
9. Elder Dempster Lines Ltd.	London—Liverpool—Hamburg—Rotterdam—Antwerp—Las Palmas—Funchal—*Dakar*—Bathurst—Bissau—Conakry—Freetown—Monrovia—Sassandra—Abidjan—Takoradi—Tema—Lomé—Cotonou—Lagos—Forcados—Burutu—Warri—Sapele—Port Harcourt—Calabar—Victoria—Tiko—Douala—Kribi—Santa Isabel—Sao Tome—Libreville New York and U.S. east coast ports—Santa Cruz de Tenerife—Las Palmas—*Dakar*—Freetown—Monrovia—Cape Palmas—Abidjan—Takoradi—Lagos—Port Harcourt—Douala
West German 10. Hanseatic Africa Line	Hamburg—Bremen—Rotterdam—Antwerp—Dunkirk—*Dakar*—Conakry—Freetown—Monrovia—Sinoe—Cape Palmas—Abidjan—Takoradi—Lomé—Cotonou—Lagos—Calabar—Douala—Libreville
11. Woermann Linie	Hamburg—Bremen—Rotterdam—Antwerp—Dunkirk—Rouen—West African ports (Las Palmas to Lobito including *Dakar*)
Dutch 12. Holland-West Afrika Lijn N.V.	Hamburg—Bremen—Amsterdam—Antwerp—Bordeaux—*Dakar*—Freetown—Monrovia (and minor Liberian ports)—Abidjan—Takoradi—Tema—Lagos—Port Harcourt—Douala—Pointe Noire—Boma—Matadi—Lobito—Luanda
13. Royal Interocean Lines N.V.	Kobe—Hong Kong—Singapore—South Africa—Douala—Port Harcourt—Lagos—Tema—Takoradi—Abidjan—Monrovia—Freetown—*Dakar*

TABLE 11 (*Continued*)

Shipping Line	*Connecting Ports*
Swiss 14. Nautilus Line, Keller Shipping S.A.	Genoa—Leghorn—Naples—Marseilles—North African ports—Taragona/Valencia—Las Palmas—*Dakar*—Freetown—Monrovia—Abidjan—Takoradi—Tema—Lomé—Cotonou—Lagos—Port Harcourt—Douala—Libreville
Norwegian 15. Høegh Lines	Oslo—Bergen—Aarhus—Copenhagen—Hamburg—Antwerp—Rouen—Casablanca—*Dakar*—Conakry—Freetown—Monrovia—Abidjan—Takoradi—Tema—Lagos—Port Harcourt—Douala—Libreville—Port Gentil—Pointe Noire
Swedish 16. Scandinavian West African Line	Gothenburg—Oslo—Bergen—Copenhagen—Antwerp—Bordeaux—*Dakar*—Freetown—Takoradi—Port Gentil
Italian 17. Italian West Africa Line	Genoa—Leghorn—Naples—Marseilles—*Dakar*—Abidjan—Takoradi—Tema—Lomé—Lagos—Sapele—Port Harcourt—Douala—Pointe Noire
18. Lloyd Triestino, S.p.A.	Trieste—Venice—Palermo—Naples—Leghorn—Genoa—Marseilles—Algiers—Casablanca—Safi—Agadir—*Dakar*—Conakry—Freetown—Monrovia—Sassandra—Abidjan—Takoradi—Tema—Lomé—Cotonou—Lagos—Port Harcourt—Douala—Libreville—Port Gentil—Pointe Noire—Matadi—Luanda—Lobito
Yugoslav 19. Jugoslavenska Linijska Plovidba (Jugolinija)	Rijeka—Split—Ploce—Genoa—Marseilles—*Dakar*—Monrovia—Abidjan—Takoradi—Tema—Lomé—Lagos—Rio de Janeiro—Santos—Montevideo—Buenos Aires

TABLE 11   (*Continued*)

Shipping Line	Connecting Ports
American	
20. Delta Line	New Orleans—*Dakar*—Conakry—Freetown—Monrovia—Abidjan—Takoradi—Tema—Lagos—Port Harcourt—Douala—Libreville—Pointe Noire—Matadi—Luanda—Lobito
21. Farrell Lines	New York—Portland—Azores—Santa Cruz de Tenerife—Las Palmas—*Dakar*—Conakry—Freetown—Monrovia—Abidjan—Takoradi—Tema—Lagos—Port Harcourt—Douala—Libreville—Pointe Noire—Matadi—Luanda—Lobito
Argentinian	
22. Argentine State Line	Argentina—Brazil—*Dakar*—Mediterranean ports
Indian	
23. Scindia Steam Navigation Co. Ltd.	Bombay—Matadi—Port Harcourt—Lagos—Takoradi—Freetown—*Dakar*—Mediterranean ports

Source: Modified from *West African Directory—1966–67* (London: Thomas Skinner & Co. (Publishers) Ltd., 1966), pp. 525–46.

of extra-West African trade in the cargo-handling pattern at the port will decrease substantially in the foreseeable future.

West African extranational coastal shipping centered at the port of Dakar is focused chiefly on the port of Abidjan in the Ivory Coast. In 1965 three per cent of the total cargo manipulations at Dakar were recorded as originating from or destined to extra-Senegalese West African ports. Of this total, 61 per cent was accounted for by the Ivory Coast.[9] Two small coastal freighters, the 996-ton *S. S. Diorhane* and the 645-ton *S. S. Avodire,* regularly service the ports of former Francophone Africa between Dakar and the port of Douala in Cameroon. In addition, service is also furnished every three weeks between Dakar and the port of Port Étienne in Mauritania by the small 282-ton *Belnabé.* However, with the recent increase in activities at Port Étienne, including the dredging of the harbor so as to be able to accommodate by direct accostage approximately 70 per cent of the ships servicing West Africa, the importance of this run has been somewhat reduced. It should also be noted that since almost all ships that service West Africa run along the entire coast, much of the extranational West African trade of Dakar is transported in this manner.

Senegalese cabotage traffic centered at Dakar is today in a state of depression owing to the improvement of road transportation facilities, the expansion of air routes, and the continued opposition to an expanded cabotage traffic by the powerful road and rail interests in Dakar. Also, with the continued expansion and improvement of the road network, it is not very likely to play a more prominent role in the future trade pattern of Senegal. In addition to the uncounted but decreasing number of small native vessels plying the Senegalese coast, cabotage traffic out of and into Dakar consists of one scheduled run: the small 1,048-ton *S. S. Ouolof* operating on a ten-day schedule between Dakar and Ziguinchor. Much of its trade was lost following the completion in 1952 of the Trans-Gambia Highway and the subsequent rapid expansion of road traffic between these two cities (see Chapter 5). Regularly scheduled cabotage service between Dakar and Saint Louis came to a close in June 1960 with the withdrawal from this run of the small 163-ton *S. S. Soulac* and her relegation to Senegal River duty. No scheduled cabotage service exists between Dakar and Kaolack, the only other relatively important port of Senegal. And finally, it should be noted that, as in the case of the extranational West African trade, much of the water-borne cargo moving between Dakar and the other ports of Senegal is carried by ships moving up and down the West African coast on their way to and from Europe and elsewhere. In 1965 Senegalese cabotage traffic accounted for less than 1 per cent of the total cargo handlings at the port.[10]

The number of lines serving Dakar and the number of ships and their total net registered tonnage calling at the port attest to its present-day international importance. In addition, despite fluctuations induced by war and economic crises, port statistics show a general increase in the number of ships calling at Dakar as well as in the total of their net registered tonnage (see Figs. 17 and 18). Much of this increase is explained by the general growth of the world's economy and the specific growth of

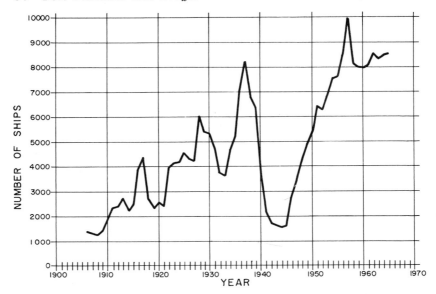

FIG. 17   Yearly movement in the number of ships calling at the Port of Dakar

that of Senegal, but much is also due to the active efforts of the Port de Commerce de Dakar, the Syndicat d'Initiative, the Chambre de Commerce, d'Agriculture et d'Industrie de Dakar, and other organizations in attracting ships and tourists to their city in lieu of neighboring competitors. Even with independence and the dissolution of French West Africa, the trend in the number of ships calling at Dakar is likely, barring another world conflict or serious economic recession, to increase in the near and foreseeable future. The growth of the economy of Senegal coupled with that of the world in general will help bring this about.

Structure of Merchandise Movements at the Port

An examination of the cargo handled by the port of Dakar shows clearly the dual nature of the port, indicates its importance as a bunkering port, and shows the importance of bunkering trade to the total structure of the port's traffic. In 1965 trade to the amount of 1,783,207 cargo tons was unloaded at the port, 49 per cent of which consisted of petroleum derivatives. In that same year 2,356,711 tons of goods (exclusive of ships' water) left the port, 37 per cent of which were re-exports of previous petroleum debarkations. In more succinct terms, most of the total of 873,212 tons of petroleum imports were re-exported in the form of ships' provisions.

Cargo other than petroleum products entering the port in 1965 amounted to 909,995 tons, and consisted primarily of foodstuffs and processed goods coming largely from France and the franc zone, a typical pattern for most colonial and ex-colonial territories (see Table 12). However, a closer examination of the total volume of unloadings at the port (including petroleum derivatives) shows a very interesting pattern: the relative and absolute importance of the Netherlands Antilles, Venezuela, and the Canary Islands as source areas for the cargo debarkations (see Fig. 19). This is explained, of course, by the fact that most of the petroleum-derivative unloadings at the port originate from refineries located in these territories. With the completion of the new refinery at Dakar,[11] this pattern will be modified considerably, with the direction of

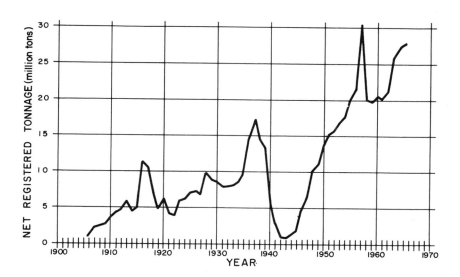

FIG. 18   Yearly movement in the net registered tonnage of ships calling at the Port of Dakar

TABLE 12   Analysis of Cargo Debarkations at the Port of Dakar for 1965

	Tons	% of Total Debarkations
Petroleum derivatives	873,212	48.97
Food, drinks, and tobacco products	558,278	31.31
Rice	177,087	
Wheat	103,692	
Millet and sorghum	27,946	
Corn	17,716	
Flour	7,949	
Sugar	98,673	
Fresh fruits and vegetables	40,173	
Fresh tuna	11,868	
Other fresh fish	6,774	
Salted and dried fish	37	
Canned fish	255	
Dairy products	15,298	
Canned fruits and vegetables	9,765	
Wine	8,063	
Beer, mineral water, and miscellaneous alcoholic drinks	9,198	
Tobacco products	2,792	
Other	20,992	
Other consumer goods	35,933	2.02
Textiles	15,655	
Automobiles	3,097	
Tires	2,522	
Other	14,659	
Agricultural raw materials	57,844	3.24
Cola nuts	21,395	
Round wood	20,312	
Sawed timber	5,086	
Tallow	3,049	
Palm oil	2,095	
Sisal	1,644	
Ginned cotton	1,083	
Other	3,180	
Mineral raw materials	32,330	1.81
Salt	20,510	
Gypsum	10,140	
Other	1,680	

TABLE 12 (*Continued*)

	Tons	% of Total Debarkations
Processed and semi-processed industrial and agricultural goods	203,049	11.39
Cement	40,023	
Fertilizer	14,857	
Construction Materials	18,165	
Paper Containers	9,232	
Other	120,772	
Miscellaneous goods	22,561	1.27
Total cargo debarkations	1,783,207˙	100.00

Source: Port Autonome de Dakar, Service des Statistiques, *Statistiques Comparées: Mois de Décembre 1965*, pp. 16–20.

trade shifting in favor of the crude-petroleum producers, notably Gabon and possibly Algeria.

In 1965 total cargo embarkations at Dakar amounted to 1,476,705 tons, of which 91 per cent consisted of peanuts, peanut derivatives, and phosphates. The balance consisted largely of products of local industries (mainly flour, cement, and processed fish) moving to other states of West Africa and the Franco-African Community and re-exports of pre-

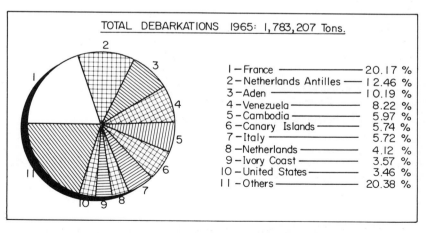

FIG. 19   Countries of origin of total debarkations for 1965

TABLE 13   Analysis of Cargo and Bunkering Embarkations at the Port of Dakar
for 1965

	Tons	% of Total Cargo Embarkations
Cargo embarkations		
Phosphates	984,944	66.70
Peanut derivatives		24.17
Peanut cake	139,486	
Decorticated peanuts	118,300	
Unrefined peanut oil	68,545	
Refined peanut oil	24,992	
Peanut bran	3,808	
Peanut flour	1,744	
Flour	21,510	1.46
Wheat	2,023	0.14
Bran	15,096	1.02
Fresh and processed fish	17,371	1.18
Tobacco products	1,403	0.10
Scrap iron	11,608	0.79
Cement	8,648	0.59
Fertilizer	1,252	0.08
Salt	10,652	0.72
Rice	6,436	0.44
Sugar	2,060	0.14
Ginned cotton	2,840	0.19
Gum arabic	4,724	0.32
Textiles	1,694	0.11
Shoes	748	0.05
Hides and skins	1,718	0.12
Other	25,103	1.70
Total cargo embarkations	1,476,705	100.00
Bunkering embarkations	880,006	
Total cargo and bunkering embarkations	2,356,711	

% of cargo embarkations to total embarkations	62.66
% of bunkering embarkations to total embarkations	37.34
	100.00

Source: Port Autonome de Dakar, Service des Statistiques, *Statistiques Comparées:
Mois de Décembre 1965*, pp. 21–25.

vious debarkations. With the important exceptions of the relatively large volume of locally manufactured and processed goods moving to other areas of tropical Africa (almost entirely a postwar phenomenon) and the petroleum-derivative unloadings and loadings, the structure of the cargo traffic moving through the port of Dakar is similar to that of most colonial and ex-colonial ports: a large volume of a few unprocessed and semi-processed raw materials moving out and processed and manufactured goods, chiefly from the colonial or ex-colonial power and associated territories, moving in (see Tables 12 and 13 and Figs. 19 and 20). However, the importance of the bunkering handlings (both absolutely and relatively) to total port handlings coupled with the volume of locally processed goods moving out of Dakar to other African markets clearly distinguishes Dakar from most other African ports. No other port of tropical Africa has such a basic cargo-manipulation mix.

The importance of intra-West African trade to the total non-bunkering cargo manipulations at the port is apparent from an examination of the West African extranational coastal shipping and Senegalese cabotage statistics. Such an examination also shows the dominant role of the port of Abidjan in this trade. In 1965 there were 69,611 tons of recorded debarkations and 35,066 tons of recorded embarkations at Dakar that orig-

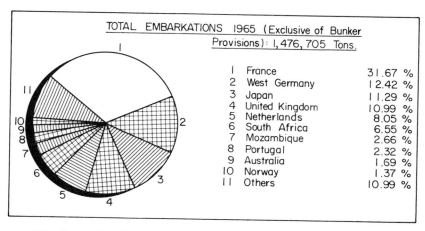

FIG. 20 Countries of destination of cargo embarkations for 1965

TABLE 14   Leading Ports of Origin of Cargo Debarkations at the Port of Dakar for 1962

	Tons	% of Total Debarkations
A. Extra-West African ports	2,050,665	
1. Western Europe	689,958	31.92
Le Havre, France	120,051	5.55
Marseilles, France	99,704	4.61
Dunkirk, France	75,337	3.49
Rotterdam, Netherlands	57,658	2.67
Rouen, France	55,885	2.59
Bordeaux, France	48,259	2.23
Milazzo, Italy	34,635	1.60
Swansea, Wales	31,905	1.48
Sète, France	27,984	1.29
Naples, Italy	21,627	1.00
Antwerp, Belgium	20,200	0.93
Lavera, France	18,291	0.85
2. Eastern Europe	363	0.02
3. Asia	142,343	6.59
Little Aden, Aden	35,042	1.62
Rangoon, Burma	33,992	1.57
Bangkok, Thailand	33,441	1.55
Saigon, South Vietnam	13,802	0.64
Pnom Penh, Cambodia	11,407	0.53
4. Anglo-America	65,814	3.05
Lake Charles, La., U.S.A.	21,936	1.01
New York, N.Y., U.S.A.	12,835	0.59
New Orleans, La., U.S.A.	10,981	0.51
Pascagoula, Miss., U.S.A.	10,499	0.49
5. Latin America	859,632	39.77
Bullen Bay, Curaçao	250,824	11.61
Oranjestad, Aruba	203,187	9.40
Punta Cardon, Venezuela	146,144	6.76
El Palito, Venezuela	126,159	5.84
Pointe-a-Pierre, Trinidad	31,716	1.47
Point Fortin, Trinidad	26,196	1.21
Amuay Bay-Las Piedras, Venezuela	18,000	0.83
Pointe-à-Pitre, Guadeloupe	14,152	0.65
Brighton, Trinidad	13,429	0.62
Puerto La Cruz, Venezuela	11,519	0.53
6. Africa (excluding West Africa)	292,555	13.54
Las Palmas, Canary Islands	103,136	4.77

TABLE 14 (*Continued*)

	Tons	% of Total Debarkations	
Santa Cruz de Tenerife, Canary Islands	68,817	3.18	
St. Vincent, Cape Verde Islands	68,320	3.16	
Casablanca, Morocco	16,718	0.77	
B. Extra-Senegalese West African ports	72,589		3.36
Abidjan, Ivory Coast	48,911	2.26	
C. Senegalese ports	11,017		0.51
D. Ships at sea	27,064		1.25
Total cargo debarkations	2,161,335		100.00

Source: République du Sénégal, Ministère des Travaux Publics et des Transports, Port de Commerce de Dakar, *Renseignements Statistiques Comparés 1962*, pp. 39–51.

inated from or were destined to other non-Senegalese West African ports. Senegalese cabotage traffic was less extensive, accounting for only 12,394 tons of recorded debarkations and 15,027 tons of recorded embarkations. In terms of percentages, this combined West African coastal trade accounted for 5 per cent of total cargo unloadings and 3 per cent of total cargo loadings at the port for that year (see Tables 16 and 17). Of the combined total volume of West African cargo handled at Dakar, approximately 60 per cent was accounted for by the port of Abidjan. The principal West African products unloaded at the port are cola nuts, tropical wood, salt, fruits and vegetables, and cotton, while converse movements consist mainly of flour, cement, rice, processed sugar, salt, refined peanut oil, fresh and processed fish, petroleum products, and textiles. However, this intra-West African trade (both extranational and cabotage) has shown a sharp decrease in recent years. The decrease in extranational West African trade is due largely to the factor of economic nationalism in other African states. The traditional export industries of Senegal (notably flour milling and cement making) are meeting direct competition from similar industries in former markets (notably the Ivory Coast) and from competition for markets from newly developed industries in other African states. The decrease in cabotage traffic is attributable largely to the fact that Dakar is today connected to Saint Louis, Kaolack, and Ziguinchor by a series of fine bituminized roads which have succeeded in

TABLE 15   Leading Ports of Destination of Cargo Embarkations at the Port of Dakar for 1962

	Tons	% of Total Embarkations
A. Extra-West African ports	844,033	
1. Western Europe	688,899	71.42
Rotterdam, Netherlands	94,381	9.78
Rouen, France	85,510	8.86
Dunkirk, France	79,688	8.26
Marseilles, France	72,267	7.49
Sète, France	67,077	6.95
Bordeaux, France	45,116	4.68
Basse-Indre, France	27,170	2.82
Nantes, France	23,289	2.41
Norrkoping, Sweden	21,223	2.20
Belfast, Northern Ireland	17,665	1.83
Bergen, Norway	11,519	1.19
Lisbon, Portugal	11,391	1.18
Brunsbuttelkoog, West Germany	10,400	1.08
2. Eastern Europe	2,074	0.22
3. Asia	52,684	5.46
Kobe, Japan	29,724	3.08
4. Anglo-America	14,628	1.52
5. Latin America	32,778	3.40
Montevideo, Uruguay	24,400	2.53
6. Africa (excluding West Africa)	52,970	5.49
Durban, South Africa	10,254	1.06
7. Oceania	12	. . .
B. Extra-Senegalese West African ports	90,518	9.38
Abidjan, Ivory Coast	57,869	6.00
Port Étienne, Mauritania	10,429	1.08
C. Senegalese ports	29,680	3.08
Ziguinchor, Senegal	27,105	2.81
D. Ships at sea	371	0.04
Total cargo embarkations	964,614	100.00

Source: République du Sénégal, Ministère des Travaux Publics et des Transports, Port de Commerce de Dakar, *Renseignements Statistiques Comparés 1962*, pp. 39–51.

TABLE 16 Extra-Senegalese West African Cargo Debarkations and Embarkations at the Port of Dakar for 1963, 1964, and 1965

A. *Debarkations*

	Tons	*% of Total Extra-Senegalese West African Cargo Debarkations*	*% of Total Cargo Debarkations*
Cola nuts	21,231	32.69	1.02
Roundwood	18,287	28.16	0.88
Sawed timber	2,674	4.12	0.13
Fruits and vegetables	6,443	9.92	0.31
Cotton	1,871	2.88	0.09
Containers	1,328	2.04	0.06
Tobacco products	747	1.15	0.04
Raw hides and skins	369	0.57	0.02
Other	11,993	18.47	0.58
Total, 1963	64,943	100.00	3.11
Total, 1964	64,273	100.00	3.36
Total, 1965	69,611	100.00	3.90

B. *Embarkations*

	Tons	*% of Total Extra-Senegalese West African Cargo Embarkations*	*% of Total Cargo Embarkations*
Flour	13,863	28.46	1.37
Salt	4,237	8.70	0.42
Petroleum products	3,726	7.65	0.37
Fresh & processed fish	2,982	6.12	0.29
Cement	1,956	4.02	0.19
Peanut oil	2,091	4.29	0.21
Textiles	1,489	3.06	0.15
Paper cartons	1,381	2.84	0.14
Shoes	1,294	2.66	0.13
Rice	1,157	2.38	0.11
Tobacco products	885	1.82	0.09
Other	13,643	28.01	1.34
Total, 1963	48,704	100.00	4.80
Total, 1964	53,963	100.00	3.86
Total, 1965	35,066	100.00	2.37

C. *Total Extra-Senegalese West African Cargo Handled*

	Tons	*% of Total Port Cargo Handlings*
Total, 1963	113,647	3.67
Total, 1964	118,236	3.57
Total, 1965	104,677	3.21

Source: (*a*) République du Sénégal, Ministère des Travaux Publics, de l'Urbanisme, de l'Habitat et des Transports, Port de Commerce de Dakar, Section de la Statistique, *Trafic Général du Mois de Décembre 1963*, pp. 28–112 and 126–196 and (*b*) Port Autonome de Dakar, Service des Statistiques, *Statistiques Comparées: Mois de Décembre 1965*, pp. 26–30.

TABLE 17   Senegalese Cabotage Cargo Debarkations and Embarkations at the Port of Dakar for 1963, 1964, and 1965

A. *Debarkations*	*Tons*	*% of Total Cabotage Cargo Debarkations*	*% of Total Cargo Debarkations*
Salt	7,710	80.13	0.37
Unrefined palm oil	601	6.25	0.03
Unrefined peanut oil	580	6.03	0.03
Wine	119	1.24	0.01
Wood	100	1.04	—
Other	512	5.32	0.02
Total, 1963	9,622	100.00	0.46
Total, 1964	21,009	100.00	1.10
Total, 1965	12,394	100.00	0.70

B. *Embarkations*	*Tons*	*% of Total Cabotage Cargo Embarkations*	*% of Total Cargo Embarkations*
Cement	8,035	31.25	0.79
Rice	6,414	24.94	0.63
Sugar	3,304	12.85	0.33
Petroleum products	1,654	6.43	0.16
Flour	1,444	5.62	0.14
Fertilizers	644	2.51	0.06
Dairy products	401	1.56	0.04
Jute and sisal sacks	319	1.24	0.03
Refined peanut oil	252	0.98	0.02
Soap	245	0.95	0.02
Wheat	153	0.60	0.02
Other	2,848	11.08	0.28
Total, 1963	25,713	100.00	2.53
Total, 1964	20,983	100.00	1.50
Total, 1965	15,027	100.00	1.02

C. *Total Cabotage Cargo Handled*	*Tons*	*% of Total Port Cargo Handlings*
Total, 1963	35,335	1.14
Total, 1964	41,992	1.27
Total, 1965	27,421	0.84

Source: (*a*) République du Sénégal, Ministère des Travaux Publics, de l'Urbanisme, de l'Habitat et des Transports, Port de Commerce de Dakar, Section de la Statistique, *Trafic Général du Mois de Décembre 1963*, pp. 28–112 and 126–96 and (*b*) Port Autonome de Dakar, Service des Statistiques, *Statistiques Comparées: Mois de Décembre 1965*, pp. 26–30.

draining much of the former cabotage traffic. Most of the existing cabotage trade is limited to high-volume, low-value commodities such as cement, salt, and rice.[12] It is very likely that this combined intra-West African trade will decrease still further in the foreseeable future unless a West African common market, as envisaged by some, materializes. Should it come about, the free flow of goods between these countries coupled with economic specialization should lead to a marked increase in this trade.

Until the changes brought about in the postwar period by the industrial boom and the introduction of phosphate exports, the basic structure of merchandise movements at the port of Dakar had remained largely unchanged since the early days of the port. However, a substantial modification of the details of such movements had taken place. Without an attempt at a detailed analysis, which will be covered in the subsequent discussion of the hinterland and its commercial outflow (see Chapter 4), it should be noted that prior to the early 1930s the composition of virtually all of Dakar's non-bunkering exports consisted of unshelled peanuts. In an effort to conserve on shipping costs, local decortication (and subsequently peanut-oil processing) was introduced. The result was a reduction of 25 to 30 per cent in volume and 65 per cent in weight of the commercially desired portion of the nut. Today, virtually no undecorticated peanuts leave Senegal for overseas markets; exports consist almost entirely of decorticated peanuts, peanut oil, and peanut oil cake. While these changes in the nature of the peanut embarkations were becoming complete in the postwar years, the two new elements of a local industry geared to a West African market (in lieu of an almost purely Senegalese one) and the appearance of phosphate exports reduced the relative (though not the absolute) importance of the peanut in the structure of merchandise movements at the port. In 1965 phosphates and the products of local industries (exclusive of peanut processing), which prior to World War II contributed virtually nothing to the embarkations at the port, accounted for approximately 70 per cent of the volume of non-bunkering embarkations.

Another change in the cargo mix of the port came about with the almost complete substitution of diesel oil for coal as the chief bunkering fuel. In 1926, the first year that separate statistics were maintained for

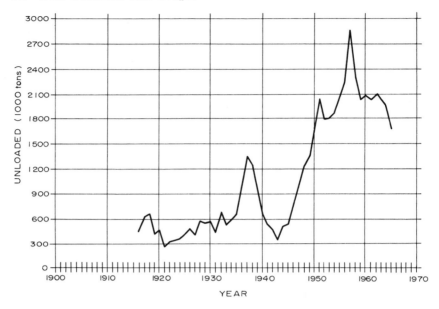

FIG. 21a   Yearly movement in total cargo debarkations at the Port of Dakar

petroleum products, a total of 900,532 tons of goods were manipulated by the port, approximately 3 per cent of which consisted of incoming and outgoing petroleum derivatives.[13] Thirty-nine years later, as has been noted, total port handlings more than quadrupled in volume, with petroleum products accounting for 42 per cent of such handlings. This increase is due, of course, not so much to the increase in the number of vessels calling at Dakar (less than double the number and less than triple the net registered tonnage) as to the almost complete changeover to diesel ships. Unfortunately, historical statistics for coal are not available, but in 1965 coal and coke imports, virtually all for local consumption, amounted to less than 1,000 tons.

Thus a study of the facilities and an analysis of the merchandise handlings at the port of Dakar clearly indicates its important role as a bunkering port, as a "colonial port" for the channeling of raw materials to the former colonial power in exchange for processed and manufactured

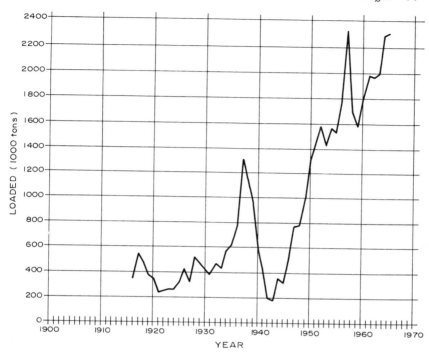

FIG. 21b Yearly movement in total cargo and bunkering embarkations at the Port of Dakar

goods, and as a West African extranational industrial center. It also reflects the positive and inhibiting factors imposed upon Dakar by the geographical elements of site and location: the former enabling it to develop into a relatively easy and safe port of call, the latter leading to its development as one of the world's foremost bunkering centers. Its location in regard to its hinterland, however, is largely a negative factor in comparison with, for example, the port of Abidjan, whose hinterland runs perpendicular to the previously enumerated east-west climatic zones of West Africa. The largely semi-arid and arid hinterland of Dakar has a much less productive agricultural potential; it is a hinterland whose principal commercial crop has been and probably will continue to be the peanut. Except for the fortuitous discovery of exportable mineral deposits (such

FIG. 22   Loading decorticated peanuts at Pier IV, Northwest Zone

as the phosphate deposits at Thiès and Taïba) which will vary the mix of Dakar's export picture to an uncertain degree, there is very little likelihood of the complete eclipse of the peanut in the overall port statistics of Dakar. And finally, the location of Dakar close to Europe (the first stop on a series of calls along the West African littoral), the relatively healthy climate for Europeans, the proximity of certain industrial raw materials, and historical impetus have led to this city's late but rapid industrial development.

Independence for the states of the West African Community has had (and, in the foreseeable future, will have) little effect upon the bunkering function of the port; Dakar will very probably continue to be (at least until the era of nuclear-powered ships) one of the world's leading bunkering centers. However, independence has set into motion a series of new forces which is in the process of modifying the role of Dakar as a "colonial port" for much of West Africa as well as an important supplier of

FIG. 23   Phosphate awaiting shipment at the Société Sénégalaise des Phosphates de Thiès Quay, Northwest Zone

manufactured goods from the Cape Verde industrial complex to extra-Senegalese markets. When these forces have run full course, it is very likely that they will have had a profound effect upon the port of Dakar by substantially modifying its traditional relationship with its economic hinterland.

4 / The Economic Hinterland

WHEN THE Federation of French West Africa was dissolved in 1959, the economic hinterland of the port of Dakar included (and was limited to) all of Senegal and most of French Sudan (present-day Mali) and Mauritania, an area of 1,800,000 square kilometers (700,000 square miles). This is still true today (see Fig. 1). Since the dissolution of the federation and political independence, however, a new set of forces has been introduced which is in the process of modifying considerably this historic relationship. It is very likely that in the future the areal extent of this hinterland will be greatly reduced and/or the hinterland's dependence upon the port of Dakar will be considerably diminished. Since these forces are largely political in nature and most changes will probably follow political lines, it is best to examine the hinterland in this context.[1]

The City of Dakar

The population of the city of Dakar is now approximately 300,000; with the inclusion of the surrounding towns and most of Cape Verde Peninsula, the population of the Dakar urban complex is close to 400,000 inhabitants. It is thus the largest city of Senegal and the West African Community (see Table 18). Like Abidjan, Conakry, Cotonou, and many of the other large cities of French-speaking West Africa, the city of Dakar is of relatively recent origin, being originally the creature of European commerce and administration with the subsequent addition of banking and industrial functions. It is today the capital city of the Republic of Senegal and, despite the natural tendency toward economic as well as political decentralization since independence, still the economic, financial, commercial, and intellectual center of much of the former federation. Most of the large private industrial, banking, and trading firms operating within French-speaking West Africa and, to a considerable extent, within former French Equatorial Africa and Cameroon still main-

TABLE 18   Urban Centers of the West African Community Having a
Population of 50,000 or Over

Urban Center	Year	Population
Senegal		
Dakar (City)	1961–1962 Census	298,280
African	1961–1962 Census	266,420
Non-African	1961–1962 Census	31,860
Dakar (Urban Complex)	1961–1962 Census	382,980
African	1961–1962 Census	344,520
Non-African	1961–1962 Census	38,460
Kaolack	1962 Estimate	81,631
Thiès	1962 Estimate	69,000
Saint Louis	1962 Estimate	58,000
Rufisque	1962 Estimate	50,000
Mali		
Bamako	1958 Census	88,500
Upper Volta		
Ouagadougou	1962 Estimate	63,000
Ivory Coast		
Abidjan	1962 Estimate	212,000
Dahomey		
Cotonou	1962 Estimate	85,845
Porto-Novo	1962 Estimate	58,800

Source: *Guid'Ouest Africain 1962–1963* (Paris: Diloutremer, 1962), pp. 2, 79, 90, 109, 122, 172, 229, 328, 402, and 406.

tain their headquarters in Dakar. In addition, the city is the home of the largest and most respected university in French-speaking Africa, the University of Dakar. In short, political independence for former French West Africa did not result in a marked decrease in the dominance of Dakar in the economic and commercial life of the Community, although in the political sphere its role was diminished from that of the political capital of the entire federation to that of the capital of Senegal. Only the city of Abidjan in the Ivory Coast, with its basically much richer hinterland, appears capable of offering a serious challenge to the preeminence of Dakar in the economic life of the Community, although the factors of tradition, historical impetus, location, and/or climate present serious and formidable obstacles in its path.

The demographic growth pattern of the city of Dakar has followed the traditional one for most large cities of former French West Africa (and many African urban centers in general): a slow but steady migration of unskilled workers from the rural areas to the city until World War II in response to its steady but unspectacular economic growth, with a massive "urban push" during the war and postwar periods. In Dakar the total population of the city increased from less than 25,000 just prior to World War I to slightly less than 100,000 at the outbreak of the second world conflict. During World War II, consumer goods were virtually unobtainable in the interior of French West Africa, being available only in the larger coastal cities, notably Dakar. This fact coupled with the relatively good wages available in newly developed local industries that were stimulated by the rupture of normal commercial ties with the Metropole resulted in a massive influx of new urban dwellers to the city. This phenomenon continued into the postwar period under the stimulus of an inflow of large amounts of private and public development and investment capital.

Today the city of Dakar is like most large African cities, with well-defined economic and social divisions. The fine residential and administrative quarter of the city is situated upon the basaltic plateau of Cape Manuel at an elevation of approximately 30 to 35 meters (see Fig. 24). Occupied principally by government buildings, apartment houses, and private residences, this section of Dakar has been designed to maximize the invigorating effect of the onshore winds which blow for approximately nine months of the year. It is a modern, well-planned, spacious, and clean quarter of the city. The commercial quarter of Dakar, with its concentration of shipping forwarders and receivers and other commercial establishments, is located in the lower reaches of the city adjacent to the port. It is the outgrowth of the original settlement at Dakar. To the northwest of "the Plateau" lies the Medina, the crowded African section of Dakar to which most of the postwar arrivals have gone. The Industrial Zone of the city is located north of the port, between the North Zone of the port and the railroad leading to the interior. With the increase in industrial activity in recent years, industries have developed beyond these limits along both the railroad and Federal Route 1 leading to Rufisque, which is itself an important industrial satellite.

Under the direction of the Service Temporaire d'Aménagement du

FIG. 24   Boulevard de la République on "le Plateau," the heart of the European residential section of Dakar

Grand Dakar, the entire peninsula of Cape Verde is now being developed in a planned and orderly manner in order to prevent the haphazard growth of the peninsula beyond the city proper. In the postwar period a fine residential area was developed at Fann; new housing developments somewhat similar to our suburban developments in the United States and which, hopefully, will eventually replace the Medina have grown under the direction of the Société Immobilière du Cap Vert (SICAP); and the impressive international airport near Yoff has succeeded in becoming the air equivalent to the port of Dakar, attracting air traffic servicing Europe and North America with South America and Africa, respectively. Its strategic location provides quick and easy contact with virtually any point in the world.

Thus the city of Dakar, profiting by and taking advantage of site, location, good climate, and that intangible Gallic charm, has developed into a fine European as well as African city, with social, cultural, and general economic amenities comparable in many ways to those of a city of the former Metropole. It is a city which, because of these amenities, has attracted the largest number of European inhabitants of any city in West Africa (approximately 10 per cent of the total population).[2]

Independence for Senegal did not result in a rapid "Africanization" of the country's commerce and civil service (as it did in Guinea and Mali, for example) and a mass exodus of expatriate residents back to the Metropole. The relatively conservative successor government that followed the disintegration of the Mali Federation in 1960 has followed a policy of gradual "Africanization," hoping that over the next decade or two, as more Senegalese are trained to assume jobs now held by Europeans, the transition can come about without a serious disruption of the nation's economy. Coupled with the continued high level of French economic and technical assistance, this concentration of a large high-income group in Dakar is reflected to a considerable extent in the nature and quantity of the cargo debarkations at the port: fresh fruit and vegetables, dairy products, wine, beer and mineral water, automobiles, and other relatively high-value consumer goods (see Table 12). Rumblings of discontent are evident, though (especially in the countryside), and should a more radical government come to power in Senegal in the near future, this could mean a program of austerity and rapid "Africanization" and repatriation, with a strong negative effect on port cargo debarkations. At the moment, this does not seem likely.

The Cape Verde Industrial Complex

As an industrial site, the Dakar–Cape Verde industrial region has certain limitations, yet it has developed into the single most important industrial agglomeration of Senegal and the West African Community. With a very limited resource base (limited almost entirely to peanuts, phosphates, limestone, and fish), no local source of energy, a limited supply of water, a questionable supply and quality of labor, and a decentralized location, Dakar and Cape Verde Peninsula have managed to outdistance Conakry (no longer within the Community) and Abidjan in industrial importance. Dakar had, however, the advantage of momentum over Abidjan, whose economic and commercial development was retarded until the creation of its port in 1950. Other advantages of Dakar include its position as the former federal capital, its fine port, its location close to important Atlantic trade routes, its relative closeness to Europe, its generally good climate for European settlement, its large and for the most part prosperous urban population, and the fact that it was (and still is) the commercial, financial, and cultural capital of most of former French Africa.

As a conditioner of the cargo handlings at the port of Dakar, the Dakar–Cape Verde industrial complex did not play an important role until World War II. Prior to the war the economies of Senegal and, to a much smaller extent, French Sudan (Mali) and Mauritania were shaped largely in the traditional colonial pattern: the export of industrial raw materials (almost entirely peanuts) in exchange for manufactured goods (chiefly textiles and hardware) from France. The basic exchange between the native producer and the trader ("traitant") was generally on a barter basis with little money passing hands; in exchange for the peanuts the grower received a line of credit at the trader's store. Only in the larger centers was an advanced money economy well developed. During this period, the cargo movements through the port of Dakar (exclusive of the bunkering trade) largely reflected this simple economic relationship: mostly peanuts moving out and generally simple manufactured goods coming in. The only important modifications in this pattern occurred during the cost-cutting depression days of the 1930s, when local decortication was introduced to reduce the weight and volume of the peanuts moving to the Metropole, and a few years earlier when a very limited amount of locally processed peanut oil was exported for the first time. This was the beginning of the present-day pattern of peanut movements, as virtually all the peanuts leaving the port of Dakar today are in the form of decorticated nuts, peanut oil, and peanut cake (see Table 13).

The first peanut-oil mill in Senegal was completed in 1920 at Diourbel by the Société Électrique et Industrielle du Baol (SEIB), with additional mills constructed in 1921 by the Société des Huileries et Rizeries de l'Ouest Africain (SHROA) at Kaolack (no longer in operation), in 1930 by the Société des Huileries et Savonneries de l'Ouest Africain (HSOA) at Dakar, in 1930 by the Société Électrique et Industrielle de

Casamance (SEIC) at Ziguinchor, in 1932 by the Établissement V. Q. Petersen at Dakar, and in 1932 by les Huileries du Cayor at Louga (no longer in operation). Until 1927 the limited amount of oil produced by the two existing mills was consumed almost entirely within Senegal, French Sudan, and Mauritania. In that year, however, the first oil exports were undertaken, and with them began the period in Senegalese economic history known as the "Bataille de l'Arachide." This battle was fought between the protectionist-minded Metropolitan producers, who were jealous of their virtual monopoly in the French market and resented the intrusion of the Senegalese oil, and the Senegalese processors. Following a period of virtually complete restrictions on processed oil imports, the Law of August 6, 1933 was passed in Paris, under the terms of which an import quota of 5,500 tons per year was allotted to the Senegalese producers. In addition, peanut-oil imports into France from other oil-producing countries were curtailed and a tariff wall was placed around Senegal to protect the local industry. Thus, although far from complete, a moderate victory was won by the then six Senegalese producers.

The quota of 5,500 tons lasted until the outbreak of World War II. Then, with the difficulties of transportation and the disruption of traditional trading patterns, the quota was raised substantially, principally to feed directly the markets of Algeria, at the time, as until recently, considered a part of the Metropole. In 1940 the quota was raised to 12,000 tons; subsequently, it was increased to 45,000 tons. It was during this period (1941) that a major Metropolitan oil producer—Lesieur—first established a mill in Senegal to take advantage of the changed conditions. Once the door was opened, it was impossible to close at the cessation of hostilities in 1945, and coupled with the implementation of the tenets of the Brazzaville Conference of 1944,[3] the immediate postwar period witnessed the arrival of two new mills: the Société de Décorticage (SODEC) at Lyndiane near Kaolack and the Compagnie Française d'Afrique Occidentale (CFAO) at Rufisque. Today there are six peanut oil-producing mills in Senegal: three on Cape Verde Peninsula (V. Q. Petersen, Lesieur, and CFAO) and three in the interior of Senegal (SEIB, SEIC, and SODEC) producing over 170,000 tons of peanut oil annually.[4]

As a conditioner of cargo movements at the ports of Senegal, the

FIG. 25   The peanut oil producing facilities of Lesieur-Afrique at Dakar

peanut-oil industry is of prime importance. While not generating any new export traffic, it modifies considerably the mix of port cargo loadings. This industry, coupled with the introduction of local decortication in the early 1930s, has resulted in a substantial change in the nature of peanut embarkations since the prewar period, with 99 per cent of the volume of peanut embarkations in 1965 consisting of decorticated peanuts, peanut oil, and peanut cake. The comparable percentage in 1939 was 38 per cent (see Table 19).

The full economic advantages of local oil processing are not immediately evident, as they are in decortication, since to a casual observer it would appear that the end result in terms of weight and volume would be the same, only the form of the decorticated peanut being altered in the pressing process. However, there are several distinct benefits to local processing. First, and perhaps foremost, are the shipping advantages. Since virtually all the oil moves to France (99 per cent in 1965), most of it moves as return cargo in tankers carrying bulk wine to West Africa. The cake, in turn, is compressed (thus reducing its volume) and shipped directly to the importing countries other than France (principally

TABLE 19   The Nature of Peanut and Peanut-Derivative Exports Passing
Through the Ports of Senegal for 1939 and 1965

	1939		*1965*[a]	
	Tons	*%*	*Tons*	*%*
Undecorticated peanuts	332,733	61.91	820	0.14
Decorticated peanuts	186,930	34.78	236,983	40.41
Peanut oil	5,107	0.95	142,634	24.32
Peanut cake	12,707	2.36	200,433	34.18
Other peanut products	. . .	. . .	5,552	0.95
Total	537,477	100.00	586,422	100.00

[a] Figures include 814 tons of undecorticated peanuts, 20,138 tons of decorticated peanuts, 90 tons of peanut oil, and 4,002 tons of peanut cake recorded as having moved on the Mali Railroad during 1965.

Sources: (a) Gouvernement Général de l'Afrique Occidentale Française, *Statistiques Mensuelles du Commerce Extérieur de l'Afrique Occidentale Française, Commerce Spécial, Importations: Exportations Décembre 1939* (Gorée: Imprimerie du Gouvernement Général, 1940), pp. 76–111; (b) République du Sénégal, Ministère du Plan et du Développement, Service de la Statistique, *Commerce Extérieur du Sénégal, Commerce Spécial, 12 Premiers Mois 1965*, pp. 1–21 (Exportations); (c) République du Mali, Ministère d'État Chargé du Plan et de la Coordination des Affaires Économiques et Financières, Service de la Statistique Générale et de la Comptabilité Économique Nationale, *Bulletin Mensuel de Statistique*, No. 1 (Janvier-Février 1966), p. 8; and (d) Interpolations by the writer.

Norway, Denmark, and Sweden in 1965), thus obviating transshipment from the French mills located largely in Bordeaux, Dunkirk, and Marseilles. Some of the cake can be (and is) retained in Senegal to supplement the meager local supplies of animal fodder. In addition, large-scale local processing provides over 2,000 jobs, lowers the local cost of the oil, and has led to the establishment of two soap producing factories catering largely to local markets.[5] Thus, instead of Senegal's being solely a supplier of an industrial raw material for the oil mills of France, many of the secondary economic benefits have accrued to its advantage.[6]

As a contributor to the cargo-loading pattern at the port of Dakar, peanut oil and peanut cake accounted for 65 per cent of the total volume of peanut and peanut-derivative embarkations and 16 per cent of the total volume of cargo loadings in 1965. Virtually all the oil and cake embarkations at the port of Dakar originated from the five mills located

TABLE 20 The Role of Peanut Oil and Peanut Cake in the Cargo Loading
Pattern of the Port of Dakar for 1965

	Tons	*% of Total Cargo Embarkations*	*% of Total Peanut and Peanut Derivative Embarkations*
Cargo embarkations	1,476,705	100.00	. . .
Peanut and peanut-derivative			
embarkations	356,875	24.17	100.00
Peanut oil	93,537	6.33	26.21
Peanut cake	139,486	9.45	39.09
Other peanut products	123,852	8.39	34.70

Source: Port Autonome de Dakar, Service des Statistiques, *Statistiques Comparées: Mois Décembre 1965*, pp. 21–25.

at Dakar, Rufisque, and Diourbel; the oil and cake from the SODEC factory at Lyndiane and the SEIC mill at Ziguinchor moved almost entirely through their local ports.[7] Thus the port of Dakar accounts for most of the oil and cake leaving Senegal for overseas markets.

Independence for Senegal has had little effect thus far on the Senegalese peanut-oil industry, which has experienced a moderate but steady growth. Output in 1965 amounted to 178,183 tons of oil (refined and unrefined), an increase of 31.6 per cent over 1959. There has been one substantial modification, however, in the peanut-oil export pattern. Prior to 1962 (the year Algeria became independent), Algeria was Senegal's second largest customer (after France), taking approximately 10 per cent of Senegal's peanut-oil exports. Today peanut-oil (and peanut) exports to independent Algeria are virtually nil; Algeria is no longer a part of France and is not within any quota and guaranteed price agreement entered into between Senegal, France, and their respective oil producers. This loss of the Algerian market has been made up by increased local consumption of oil and by a rise in the exports to France. After a sharp decline in 1962 and 1963, oil exports in 1964 and 1965 were above the 1961 level.

The future for the Senegalese peanut-oil industry (and consequently movements of oil and cake through the port of Dakar) is very prob-

TABLE 21   The Role of the Port of Dakar in Total Peanut and Peanut-Derivative Embarkations at the Ports of Senegal for 1965

	Total Embarkations[a] at the Ports of Senegal (tons)	Total Embarkations at the Port of Dakar (tons)	% of Total Passing Through Dakar
Undecorticated peanuts	820	0	0.00
Decorticated peanuts	236,983	118,300	49.92
Peanut oil	142,634	93,537	65.58
Peanut cake	200,433	139,486	69.59
Other peanut products	5,552	5,552	100.00
	586,422	356,875	

[a] Figures include 814 tons of undecorticated peanuts, 20,138 tons of decorticated peanuts, 90 tons of peanut oil, and 4,002 tons of peanut cake recorded as having moved on the Mali Railroad during 1965.

Sources: (a) République du Sénégal, Ministère du Plan et du Développement, Service de la Statistique, *Commerce Extérieur du Sénégal, Commerce Spécial, 12 Premiers Mois 1965*, pp. 1–21 (Exportations); (b) République du Mali, Ministère d'État Chargé du Plan et de la Coordination des Affaires Économiques et Financières, Service de la Statistique Générale et de la Comptabilité Économique Nationale, *Bulletin Mensuel de Statistique*, No. 1 (Janvier-Février 1966), p. 8; (c) Port Autonome de Dakar, Service des Statistiques, *Statistiques Comparées: Mois de Décembre 1965*, pp. 21–25; and (d) Interpolations by the writer.

lematical. The big uncertainty is the effect that the Convention of Association with the European Economic Community that Senegal signed in July 1963 (the Yaoundé Convention), and which came into force in June 1964, will have upon the industry. Until the 1964–1965 peanut season,[8] peanut-oil exports to France (99 per cent of the oil exports in 1964 and 1965) were covered by a yearly quota agreement entered into among Senegal, France, and the oil processors of both countries. A certain portion of the quota was to be satisfied by the export of decorticated peanuts at prices, guaranteed by France, well above the world market prices; the balance in refined and unrefined peanut oil at prices agreed upon by the French and Senegalese oil producers. Under the terms of the Convention of Association, Senegalese peanut oil is to move into the Common Market quota-free and duty-free, but under competitive market conditions. Since one study[9] showed that the agreed price for Senegalese oil produced during the 1963–1964 peanut year was 38 per

TABLE 22   Senegalese Peanut-Oil Production and Exports for 1959–1965
(*In Thousands of Metric Tons*)

	1959	1960	1961	1962	1963	1964	1965
Production							
Unrefined oil	99	106	117	107	105	119	120
Refined oil	36	38	36	46	53	56	58
Total	135	144	153	153	158	175	178
Exports							
Unrefined oil	99	101	114	103	78	103	118
Refined oil	15	13	12	16	26	26	24
Total	114	114	126	119	104	129	142

Sources: (*a*) République du Sénégal, Commissariat Général au Plan, Service de la Statistique et de la Mécanographie, *Bulletin Statistique et Économique*, Année 1962, No. 7 (Juillet 1962) (Dakar: Grande Imprimerie Africaine), pp. 6 and 26; (*b*) République du Sénégal, Ministère du Plan et du Développement, Service de la Statistique, *Bulletin Statistique et Économique Mensuel*, Année 1963, No. 12 (Décembre 1963) (Dakar: Grande Imprimerie Africaine), pp. 6 and 28; and (*c*) République du Sénégal, Ministère du Plan et du Développement, Service de la Statistique, *Bulletin Statistique et Économique Mensuel*, Année 1966, No. 5 et 6 (Mai-Juin 1966) (Dakar: Grande Imprimerie Africaine), pp. 6 and 28.

cent above the average world market price for the previous three years, there is some uncertainty (even with tariff protection) as to the future competitive position of this industry under the new conditions.

An additional uncertainty was provided by Nigeria's application for associate membership with the Common Market. Under the terms of the Brussels agreement signed in July 1965, however, Nigerian peanut oil entering the Common Market until 1969 will be subject to a duty-free quota—a quota based upon preagreement peanut-oil exports to the six European states. This quota was and will continue to be raised 3 per cent annually effective 1965 (although association did not come into effect until 1966). All Nigerian peanut oil entering the Common Market above the quota will be subject to normal tariff rates. Because of this safeguard plus the traditional ties with French oil producers, the opportunity to sell within tariff walls to a much larger market, and a growing African market, the Senegalese oil industry is generally optimistic. Under the terms of the Second Development Plan which came into operation on July 1, 1965, peanut-oil production is to increase at approximately the same rate as peanut production—5 per cent annually. Thus, barring unforeseen eventualities, it is very probable that peanut-oil (and cake) movements through the port of Dakar will increase in the coming years; an average growth rate of 5 per cent per annum would appear to be a fair estimate.

The second most important industry conditioning the cargo embarkation pattern at the port of Dakar is flour milling. In 1965 it accounted for approximately 2.5 per cent of the volume of port cargo embarkations: 21,510 tons of flour (destined almost entirely to Malagasy, Gabon, Central African Republic, Chad, and Guinea) and 15,096 tons of bran (chiefly to the fodder-deficient nations of western Europe). In addition, it accounted for 103,692 tons of wheat debarkations at the port (see Tables 12 and 13). Unlike the peanut-oil industry, flour milling is not based on a local raw material, with the result that flour and bran exports are double-counted in port statistics, wheat coming in and flour and bran moving out.

The first flour mill in Senegal was constructed in 1953 at Dakar by the Moulins Sentenac; a year later, a second flour mill was constructed (also at Dakar) by the Grands Moulins de Dakar.[10] Their location at Dakar was conditioned by the large local bread-consuming market plus the ease of transshipment to the rest of French West Africa, French Equatorial Africa, Togo, and Cameroon; their combined total capacity (150,000 tons of wheat or 110,000 tons of flour annually) was designed with these markets in mind. To assure their economic success, France subsidized the cost of wheat moving to these mills and agreed to divide the sub-Saharan French African flour market with them (75 per cent for the Senegalese mills, 25 per cent for the mills of France). With independence, these agreements are no longer in force. An additional negative factor has been the construction in 1963 of a new flour mill at Abidjan in the Ivory Coast by the Grands Moulins d'Abidjan. With this increased competition (the Ivory Coast alone accounted for over 30,000 tons of flour embarkations at the port of Dakar in 1962), the traditional markets for Senegalese flour have been greatly reduced, and today these mills are running at approximately 50 per cent of capacity.

Owing to the existence of flour mills in many of the countries of West Africa (the Ivory Coast, Sierra Leone, Ghana, and Nigeria) plus competition from extra-African producers, it is not very likely that flour exports (and consequently flour embarkations at the port of Dakar) will increase substantially in the foreseeable future. In the coming years, production increases in the Dakar mills will be dependent largely upon an increase in the domestic consumption of wheat flour as urbanism and living standards increase in Senegal. Extra-Senegalese export markets for the flour will be limited largely to neighboring countries such as Mali and Mauritania plus a limited amount to other African markets. Therefore, while wheat imports (in the past almost entirely from France) will probably rise, flour exports and port flour embarkations should remain close to their present-day depressed levels. Bran production will increase as flour production rises, but the development of a local poultry industry near Dakar, Saint Louis, and Thiès could (and probably will) absorb most of this increased output.

In 1965 the tuna-canning industry provided 4,986 tons of cargo embarkations at the port of Dakar; an additional 348 tons were provided by other canned edible fish. This total represented 31 per cent of all fresh- and processed-fish embarkations and 0.4 per cent of total cargo embarkations for the year. Most of this canned fish was destined for France (97 per cent of the total canned-fish embarkations). Until the 1964 season, this industry, especially tuna canning, was perhaps the fastest-growing industry in Senegal, with 1963 production being two and one-quarter times greater than the 1959 output.[11] Unfortunately, 1964 was, in terms of tuna catch, a very poor year, with a 23 per cent decrease recorded in canned fish output.[12] With twenty fewer French tuna boats returning for the 1965 season,[13] this industry appears to be in a temporary recession.

Until 1953 virtually all the fish caught in the coastal waters of Senegal (estimated at 50,000 tons annually) were brought in by approximately 10,000 to 15,000 native fishermen using native canoes (pirogues). Approximately one-third of the total catch was smoked, salted, or dried and shipped to various West African markets. In that year studies were undertaken along the coasts of French West Africa which indicated that these coastal waters (and in particular those of Senegal) were rich in edible fish, notably the yellow-fin tuna. Taking note of these studies, the Comptoir Français de l'Industrie des Conserves Alimentaires (COFICA), a purchasing agent for French fish canneries, sent two fishing boats to these waters during the 1955 season. Having confirmed the findings of the studies, a Senegalese subsidiary of COFICA was organized, the Comptoir Sénégalais de l'Industrie des Conserves Alimentaires (COSICA), and six tuna boats were sent to Senegalese waters during the 1956 tuna season. This same season witnessed the construction of the first fish cannery at Dakar. At first most of the tuna was shipped frozen to France, but by 1960, with seven small French-owned canneries in operation, virtually all was processed at Dakar. By 1963 there were over sixty French and Senegalese tuna boats operating out of Dakar, with an annual catch of close to 20,000 tons.

Tuna fishing has received a great deal of emphasis in the development plans of Senegal, not only in terms of canning but also in the export of frozen fish to foreign canneries. In 1965, in addition to the canned-fish exports, frozen-tuna embarkations at the port of Dakar amounted to 8,556 tons, 10 per cent of which went to American canneries in Puerto Rico (frozen tuna was the leading Senegalese export to the United States), with most of the remainder going to European processors. The First Four Year Development Plan envisaged a tuna catch of 40,000 tons during the 1965 tuna-fishing season (a goal not achieved), and it shows the optimism of the Senegalese planners in this field:

The sale of tuna on the European market (capable of absorbing more than 150,000 tons by 1964) and on the American market ought not to present any difficulties, even if similar industries are set up in other countries of West Africa. Senegal has certain appreciable advantages: a favorable climate, an efficient and skilled labor force, and a fine port with good facilities.[14]

Despite the fact that the planned goal was not achieved, the exports of canned and frozen tuna are very likely to increase in the coming years, with a consequent increase in tuna embarkations at the port of Dakar. To this end two notable events have taken place. The first of these occurred early in 1963 when the Société Frigorifique du Sénégal (SOFRIGAL) was formed. This company was organized jointly by an American concern, Starkist Foods, Inc., a French company, the Société Armement André Dhellemmes, and the Banque Sénégalaise de Développement (BSD), with participation ratios of 32.5 per cent, 32.5

per cent, and 35 per cent, respectively, to construct and operate a new fish-freezing plant in the new fishing zone of the port (which was recently constructed with help from the Development Fund of the European Economic Community). With a loan of 400,000 dollars from the American Export-Import Bank, the new plant was opened on January 28, 1964, with a capacity of 50,000 tons of fish. The second event took place in March 1965, when an agreement was signed between the Senegalese and Soviet governments for the construction of a new tuna cannery, also in the new fishing zone. When completed in the indefinite future, this plant will have a daily capacity of approximately 100 tons and will replace the existing small and poorly equipped canneries.

However, two questions remain. Can enough tuna be caught and unloaded at Dakar to satisfy the needs of this industry? Can markets be found for the planned increase in output? If there is sufficient tuna in coastal waters, the first question can be resolved by increased investments in a national tuna fleet, which is what is planned. The second question is much more problematical. Since canned tuna is a relatively high-cost commodity, the African market will by necessity be limited; the principal outlets will have to be in Europe and North America. In this respect, Senegal's association with the European Economic Community will be a decided advantage. The West African tuna waters, however, are not restricted to Senegal; this fish is found along most of the western coast of Africa. In virtually all the coastal countries of West Africa (for example, Nigeria, Ghana, the Ivory Coast, Guinea, and even the Gambia) post-independence development plans call for the development or expansion of commercial fishing operations, including tuna processing (another factor limiting the African market for Senegalese tuna). Such increased competition (along with American, European, and Japanese producers) for the rather limited world tuna market will present certain difficulties to the fulfillment of Senegal's development plans. This industry, though, now appears to be strongly implanted in Senegal, has shown a remarkable growth over the past decade (despite the recent slump), and will very likely increase still further in the coming years. All of this bodes well for future tuna debarkations and embarkations at the port of Dakar, which is already the leading tuna port of France and the French Community.

The cement industry located at Bargny near Rufisque accounted for 8,648 tons of cargo embarkations at the port of Dakar during 1965. However, virtually all of these loadings were cabotage movements to other Senegalese coastal points, mainly the port of Ziguinchor in Casamance. The virtual disappearance of extra-Senegalese cement embarkations at the port of Dakar represents a considerable drop from the pre-independence and immediate post-independence statistics, when exports to the other territories and countries of French-speaking West Africa alone (notably the Ivory Coast) generally amounted to 10,000 to 20,000 tons. This loss of the West African market is due not so much to competition from local cement factories in the other countries (the Ivory Coast does not yet have a cement plant) as to competition from European and other African producers. Local consumption of cement nevertheless has managed to make up largely for the loss of the West African market (the plant is running at more than 90 per cent of capacity).

Studies for the construction of a cement plant near the limestone deposits at Bargny were first undertaken in 1942 by the Société Ouest Africaine des Ciments (SOCOCIM). The extent of the deposits plus

FIG. 26　The Société Ouest Africaine des Ciments (SOCOCIM) cement plant at Bargny, near Rufisque

their location near the main Dakar-Thiès road and their proximity to the main line of the Dakar-Niger Railroad led to a favorable report. Work on the project was started in 1942, but because of war-induced delays it was not completed until 1948. Initial capacity of the plant was 60,000 tons; it was subsequently raised to 120,000 tons in 1954 and 200,000 tons in 1960, its present-day capacity. The object of the plant was to supply much of the cement market in French West Africa, French Equatorial Africa, Togo, and Cameroon. With independence and the loss of much of this guaranteed market, sales are today mainly limited to Senegal (over 90 per cent of the output in 1965).

It is very unlikely that cement embarkations at the port of Dakar in the foreseeable future will approach their pre-independence level. Even if a true West African customs union should evolve eventually, it is very likely that many (if not most) of these countries will have their own competitive industry. Although economically questionable in many cases, cement plants exist or are planned, in addition to Senegal, in at least Mali, Upper Volta, the Ivory Coast, Togo, Ghana, and Nigeria. Thus the future for the SOCOCIM plant appears to be tied to the local Senegalese market plus exports to neighboring countries, especially Mali (currently getting much of its cement from the Soviet bloc) and Mauritania. Cement movements through the port of Dakar will probably continue to reflect the current pattern: a limited amount of embarkations for extra-Senegalese markets (notably Mauritania), with cabotage movements playing a relatively important role.

Senegal also has a cotton-textile industry concentrated close to the principal markets on Cape Verde Peninsula which conditions cargo movements through the port of Dakar to a limited extent. This industry consists of four principal mills, all of which were started after 1952: (1) the Industrie Cotonnière Africaine (ICOTAF), which spins thread and weaves cloth; (2) the Manufactures de Rufisque, solely a thread-spinning mill; (3) the Compagnie Cotonnière du Cap-Vert, a weaver of cloth; and (4) the Société Cotonnière Transocéanique, a weaver of cloth. In 1965 production amounted to 330 tons of thread, 1,131 tons of plain cotton cloth, and 269 tons of printed goods, all far below the level set in the First Four Year Development Plan. In addition to these four principal mills, over a dozen small firms turn out ready-made clothing such as shirts, blouses, and pants. The spinning and weaving industry depends to a considerable extent upon imported raw cotton, mainly from other West African countries: Niger, Upper Volta, the Ivory Coast, Dahomey, Nigeria, and, now that economic relations have been restored, Mali. In 1965 a total of 1,083 tons of raw cotton was recorded as having been unloaded at the port of Dakar.

Although prior to independence approximately 10 per cent of the output of the Cape Verde cotton-textile industry was exported (chiefly to the countries of French-speaking West and Equatorial Africa), this figure has now been cut in half because of increased competition in these traditional markets.[15] In this regard the embarkation figure of 1,694 tons of textile loadings at the port of Dakar for 1965 should be read carefully, for most of it consists of transshipped textile goods passing through Dakar. Since this is one of the first industries that many economically developing countries establish, it is very unlikely that Senegalese textile exports (and consequently port embarkations) will increase substantially in the foreseeable future. Like those of cement and flour, its future markets outside Senegal appear limited largely to Mali and Mauritania. Since the Senegalese textile industry currently supplies approximately one-half of its domestic needs, however, an expansion in production to increase this percentage could result in increased cotton debarkations at the port of Dakar, although increased imports from Mali and/or the development of domestic cotton production (as is planned) could limit such a possibility.

Another somewhat related industry which is also located in the Dakar–Cape Verde industrial complex is the manufacturing of sisal twine and bags. Sisal fiber is imported (2,372 tons in 1965, chiefly from Brazil, Malagasy, and Kenya) and twine is produced. This, in turn, is used for making sacks for peanuts and other commodities, rope and cord for fishermen, and rugs. The Société Commerciale et Industrielle du Sac (SOCOSAC), founded in 1938, is engaged in these operations, and it accounted for 485 tons of cargo embarkations at the port of Dakar in 1965.

The Société Africaine Bata shoe factory at Rufisque accounted for 748 tons of cargo embarkations at the port of Dakar in 1965. A subsidiary of the international Bata chain of shoe factories, this plant was

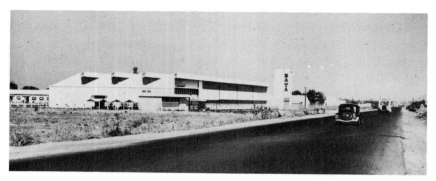

FIG. 27   The Bata shoe factory at Rufisque

established in Senegal in 1941 with its own tannery (processing West African leather), shoemaker's school, and assembly line, with sales outlets mainly in French-speaking West and Equatorial Africa. Production increased steadily from 200,000 pairs of shoes and sandals at the outset to almost 4,000,000 pairs in 1965. Most of the unit production today, however, is in the form of inexpensive plastic shoes and sandals which have little value but find a large African market. In 1963 the largest non-Senegalese customer was the Ivory Coast, which accounted for over 50 per cent of the shoe embarkations at the port of Dakar. With the completion of a new Bata plant at Abidjan in the Ivory Coast in 1964 (plus competitive industries elsewhere in West Africa), production at the Rufisque plant in 1964 was down 16 per cent from the preceding year, while 1965 production figures decreased still further, output for that year being equivalent to 68 per cent of the 1963 production figures.[16]

Although not conditioning the cargo-embarkation pattern at the port of Dakar to any appreciable degree, the new petroleum refinery constructed by the Société Africaine de Raffinage (SAR) at M'Bao, 18 kilometers north of the port proper on Gorée Bay, will have a profound effect upon the cargo-debarkation pattern at the port. Prior to its construction (its first stage was put into operation in January 1964), all the petroleum debarkations at the port were in the form of petroleum derivatives (fuel oil, diesel oil, gasoline, kerosene, etc.) coming mainly from the refineries of Latin America, Aden, and the Canary Islands.

With the completion of the first stage of the refinery (capacity 600,000 tons), 283,578 tons of crude oil from Algeria and Gabon were unloaded directly at the refinery in 1965. Virtually all of the products produced there were locally consumed and did not directly effect the cargo movements at the port, although they did have the indirect effect of reducing refined petroleum debarkations, notably gasoline. When the final stage of the refinery is completed in the undetermined future, it will have a total capacity of 1,200,000 tons, and most of the petroleum debarkations will then be at M'Bao in the unrefined state. Since the Senegalese market, with its large bunkering trade, will be able to absorb virtually all the refinery's output, only a very limited amount will leave Senegal for other West African markets, notably Mali and Mauritania.

In addition to the above industries which directly condition the cargo-movement pattern at the port of Dakar to a considerable extent, the Dakar–Cape Verde industrial complex has many other industries whose influence upon port cargo movements is much more limited. Many of these, however, are also directly or indirectly dependent upon the port. Note should be made of the following:

1. Food and beverage industries—include eight breweries and carbonated beverage producers, four sea-biscuit plants, four candy factories, a plant producing lump sugar from imported granular sugar, and numerous bakeries;

2. Chemical industries—include a match factory, a factory producing pharmaceuticals (cough drops and patent medicines), a producer of liquid oxygen, three paint factories, an explosives manufacturer, a maker of household disinfectants, a battery maker, and a producer of carbon dioxide; and

3. Miscellaneous industries—include sawmills, cigarette manufacturing, brick works, a maker of fluorescent lights, two makers of metal containers, an air-conditioning unit assembly plant, metal and wooden furniture makers, a truck assembly plant, an assembly plant for simple farm equipment, and, of course, a thermal power plant.

Although not in the Dakar–Cape Verde industrial complex, future development plans call for the construction of a superphosphate fertilizer plant by the Société Industrielle d'Engrais au Sénégal (SIES) near the phosphate-mining operations of the Compagnie Sénégalaise des Phosphates de Taïba north of Thiès. When completed by 1968 this joint public-private venture will have an initial capacity of 60,000 tons (eventual capacity: 130,000 tons) of fertilizer and should provide a minimum of 10,000 tons of fertilizer embarkations at the port of Dakar. In addition to this operation, future plans call for the construction of a new pharmaceutical factory, a plywood plant, and a meat cannery.

Independence for the territories of former French West Africa has had a marked effect upon the industries of the Cape Verde industrial complex. Prior to 1960 this was the leading industrial agglomeration of the entire federation, basing its impressive development largely upon two principal industrial locational factors: raw materials and markets. The former accounted for the development of the peanut-oil processing industry and the embryonic tuna canneries, while virtually all of the other industries were market oriented. For many industries, however, the market factor was interpreted broadly and was not limited to Senegal (and especially the Dakar–Cape Verde region) but included a protected market that comprised all of French West Africa and to a lesser extent French Equatorial Africa, Togo, and Cameroon. In addition Dakar also offered secondary benefits to potential private investors: it was a modern and in many ways a European city offering many of the amenities of an urban center in the Metropole; it was the political, cultural, and commercial capital of French West Africa; it had a fairly good climate; and it was the closest large French-African city to Europe. This last factor, while it offered easy movement to the Metropole, also was advantageous from an industrial viewpoint for obviating back haulage upon goods processed in Africa for an African market but drawing the basic raw materials from Europe (for example, flour milling). Thus by 1959 Dakar had, in terms of value of industrial production, a lead five times greater than its nearest industrial competitor, Abidjan, and was an important industrial supplier for much of French-speaking Africa.[17]

With independence came two important new developments: the loss of French-guaranteed extra-Senegalese African markets for Senegalese industries, and the development of competitive industries in other countries of Africa, notably the Ivory Coast. In addition the loss of much of the Guinean market (no longer in the franc monetary bloc) and the temporary loss of the Malian market had a negative effect upon Senegalese industrial development. Thus by 1964 those Senegalese industries that developed a large extra-Senegalese African market found their traditional outlets curtailed. The biggest single factor was the rapid development of industry in the Ivory Coast, traditionally the largest market by far for Senegalese intra-African industrial exports. Although still far behind Dakar in industrial development, Abidjan, with its booming economy and rapid growth, is making impressive strides in the industrial field. In a study prepared in 1964 comparing the growth rates of the industrial sectors of the economies of Senegal and the Ivory Coast,[18] it was shown that between 1959 and 1962 the value of industrial output in both countries increased; but whereas Senegalese industrial output went up approximately 25 per cent, the increase for the equivalent period in the Ivory Coast was slightly less than 100 per cent. In these three years the ratio of industrial output between Senegal and the Ivory Coast decreased from 5:1 to 3:1 in favor of Senegal. It is very likely that this ratio is even less today.

Some of the competitive industries that have been developed or are in the process of being developed in the Ivory Coast include flour milling, oil refining, vegetable-oil extraction (palm oil), the assembling of trucks and farm equipment, and the production of soap, matches, metal drums, textiles and clothing, shoes, and sisal twine and sacks. As a result cargo embarkations at the port of Dakar from the industries of Cape Verde destined for the Ivory Coast, which amounted to over 50,000 tons annually before independence, are today less than 10,000 tons. On a more limited scale other competitive industries are in existence (or contemplated) in other states of the West African Community and elsewhere in traditional Senegalese African markets, which have further reduced (or will reduce) these markets. Unless a true West African customs union is developed (the Union Douanière des États de l'Afrique de l'Ouest has never been fully implanted) and industrial specialization is practiced, it appears very unlikely that the Cape Verde industrial complex will recapture much of its former pre-eminence as a supplier of manufactured goods to much of West and Equatorial Africa. Its future appears to be limited largely to processing local raw materials for export to extra-African markets (peanut-oil processing and tuna canning) and to supplying the needs of Senegal and a few neighboring states, notably Mali and Mauritania, with limited exports to other African markets. This has already been reflected in the decrease of extra-Senegalese West African cargo embarkations at the port of Dakar in the post-independence period (see Chapter 3).

The Senegalese Hinterland

Although Cape Verde Peninsula is important as a conditioner of cargo movements at the port of Dakar by providing the largest and most prosperous market and the leading industrial region of the French West African Community, it is from beyond the peninsula that the port draws the vast bulk of the commodities that pass through it either with little or no prior processing or after an intensive physical change in form (for example, peanut-oil extraction). Although the Dakar hinterland includes all of Senegal and most of Mali and Mauritania, it is from Senegal that the port draws most of its cargo embarkations. In terms of specific commodities, it is Senegal that provides all the phosphate loadings and over 90 per cent of the peanut and peanut-derivative embarkations at the port of Dakar. In 1965 these two catagories accounted for 91 per cent of the total volume of cargo embarkations at the port (see Table 13) and for 95 per cent and 87 per cent, respectively, of the total volume and value of Senegalese exports (see Table 24). Of the two, peanuts, while contributing a smaller volume of port cargo embarkations than phosphates, are the most important by far in terms of value of Senegalese exports (79 per cent in 1965) as well as in terms of historical importance, being the most important export of Senegal for over one hundred years.

The importance of peanuts to the export economy of Senegal dates from shortly after the return of Senegal to France by the English following the signing of the Treaty of Vienna of 1815. Prior to this time, the importance of Senegal was measured in terms of a commercial barter economy: the exchange of simple manufactured goods for gum arabic, ostrich feathers, skins, ivory, gold, and slaves (see Chapter 2). By the time of the colony's return to France, modern industrialism had taken hold in western Europe, and with it came a search for new, overseas sources of raw cotton, oil seeds, indigo and other dyes, and other basic industrial goods and the converse search for markets. The early history

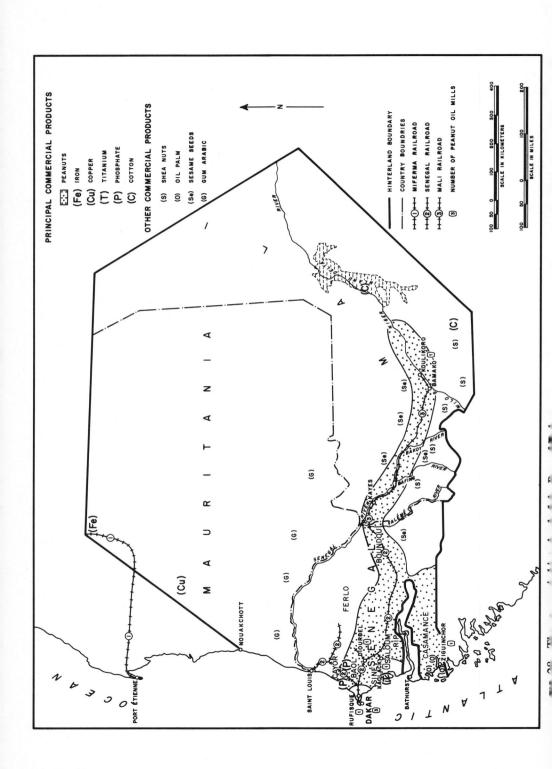

TABLE 23   Volume of Principal Exports from Senegal, French Sudan, and Mauritania for 1939, 1948, and 1958

(In Metric Tons)

Commodities	1939	1948	1958
Decorticated peanuts	186,930	199,535	329,599
Undecorticated peanuts	332,733	1,256	96
Peanut oil	5,107	49,083	107,289
Peanut cake	12,707	67,690	144,878
Aluminum phosphate	. . .	. . .	43,663
Gum arabic	5,556	6,343	5,627
Fish (salted, dried, and smoked)	677	3,846	3,585
Palm kernels	3,709	3,287	2,296
Shea kernels	1,903	30,882	316
Shea butter	392	1,619	1,654
Oil cake (except peanut)	60	131	2,626
Hides and skins	1,297	542	1,485
Live animals	240	432	556
Kapok	691	695	208
Raw wool	404	40	107
Raw cotton	448	45	20
Green coffee	1	169	103
Titanium and zirconium ores	1,492	2,680	. . .
Rice	46	192	. . .
Beeswax	182	110	. . .
Meat (fresh, frozen, and salted)	233	105	. . .
Other commodities	6,277	20,116	104,402
Total exports	561,085	388,798	748,510

Sources: (a) Gouvernement Général de l'Afrique Occidentale Française, *Statistiques Mensuelles du Commerce Extérieur de l'Afrique Occidentale Française, Commerce Spécial, Importations: Exportations Décembre 1939* (Gorée: Imprimerie du Gouvernement Général, 1940), pp. 76–111; (b) Gouvernement Général de l'Afrique Occidentale Française, *Statistiques du Commerce Extérieur de l'Afrique Occidentale Française, Commerce Spécial, Importations: Exportations, Année 1948* (Rufisque: Imprimerie du Gouvernement Général, 1949), pp. 68–99; and (c) Haut Commissariat Général à Dakar, Études et Coordination Statistiques et Mécanographiques, *Bulletin Statistique et Économique Mensuel*, Avril 1959, No. 4, p 6.

of Senegal following its return to France reflects this change. Although the tradtional commercial pattern had largely been reinstated (with the exception, of course, of slavery), the early colonial governors, under orders of the new royal government, undertook intensive studies of the agricultural potentialities of the colony.

TABLE 24   Volume and Value of Principal Exports from Senegal for 1965
(Metric Tons and 1,000,000 Francs CFA)

Commodity	Volume	%	Value	%
Peanuts and peanut derivatives		37.1		78.6
Decorticated peanuts	216,845		9,217	
Undecorticated peanuts	6		. . .	
Peanut oil	142,544		13,143	
Peanut cake	196,431		2,553	
Phosphates		58.1		8.5
Calcium phosphate	767,137		2,373	
Aluminum phosphate	99,900		296	
Phosphate fertilizer	4,041		21	
Bran	20,228	1.3	232	0.7
Flour	19,756	1.3	690	2.2
Salt	6,144	0.4	24	0.1
Canned fish	5,536	0.4	1,113	3.5
Palm kernels	3,757	0.3	111	0.4
Scrap iron	3,013	0.2	27	0.1
Gum arabic	2,216	0.1	185	0.6
Hides and skins	1,379	0.1	184	0.6
Steel containers	896	0.1	150	0.5
Fish (fresh, salted, dried, and smoked)	490	. . .	46	0.1
Sisal sacks	266	. . .	24	0.1
Cotton textiles	126	. . .	77	0.2
Shoes	113	. . .	71	0.2
Other commodities	8,377	0.6	1,175	3.7
Total exports	1,499,201	100.0	31,712	100.0

Note: 245 francs CFA equals one U.S. dollar.
Source: République du Sénégal, Ministère du Plan et du Développement, Service de la Statistique, *Bulletin Statistique et Économique Mensuel*, Année 1966, No. 5 et 6 (Mai-Juin 1966) (Dakar: Grande Imprimerie Africaine, 1966), pp. 28 and 29.

The new colonial relationship was defined clearly in the orders received by Governor Jacques-François Roger upon his departure for Saint Louis in 1821 to assume his new office:

Go and create for France a colony which will furnish it at least some of the commodities for which it is now dependent upon foreign sources and which will offer France a large outlet for the products of its industries; create large agricultural schemes and grow vegetables of both worlds upon a soil which up to now has produced very little; carry to the people of Senegal, with new needs and new pleasures, the taste of work; and with work, to help them spread civilization to the far interior of Africa.[19]

Governor Roger, like his two predecessors, governors Le Coupé and Schmaltz, but on a larger scale, brought in specialists from France, botanists, gardeners, surveyors, chemists, engineers, and others to study the economic potentialities of the colony. Perhaps the most famous and lasting legacy of this period was the establishment of an experimental agricultural station on the left bank of the Senegal River 170 kilometers upstream from Saint Louis by the botanist-gardener Richard, to which he gave the name Richard-Toll ("toll" means garden in the Wolof language). At this and other stations, soils were tested, hydrographic and geologic studies were made, and tropical and middle-latitude crops were grown on an experimental basis: cotton, indigo, annatto (the source of an orange dye), kapok, tobacco, onions, pimentoes, bananas, papaya, sugar cane, tea, coffee, cacao, sesame, castor plant, tropical wood, pine trees, rubber, peanuts, millet, rice, and other crops. Cotton and indigo received the greatest attention, with small European plantations and native holdings soon established near Saint Louis and in the Senegal River Valley. However, cotton exports to France reached only 50 tons between 1822 and 1825, and the cost was very high; the severe sahelian climate, the sandy soil, and floods had taken their toll. By 1826 the continuation of these development plans had caused much controversy (many had grown disillusioned with the expenditures in the colony and the slow, if any, progress being made), and Governor Roger asked to be recalled.

Pending the appointment of a permanent successor, the Ministère de la Marine et des Colonies sent an interim governor to Senegal to study the problem and to send back information as to "the soil resources and the disposition of the black race toward work and toward agriculture, on the basis of which the central government will decide whether to continue the sacrifices necessary to make Senegal a true colony or if Senegal should revert to solely a trading territory." [20] In 1827 Interim-Governor Gerbidon wrote to his ministry:

Experience has not confirmed the hopes conceived [by the previous governors], and Senegal does not appear ever to be destined as an agricultural colony. . . . Senegal, despite truly extraordinary vegetation during the rainy season, has only a superficial appearance of fertility. . . . The soil is not good for agriculture, it is almost everywhere saline, and the floods fertilize only a very limited amount of the country. . . . The climate, especially, produces disastrous effects. The east wind, which arrives in Senegal with all the aridity of the desert and burns what it crosses, kills even the most hardy vegetation all of a sudden. The rains fall only during four months of the year and on the average for only 23 days, and consequently it is impossible to develop large-scale irrigation schemes without the expenditure of a great deal of capital.[21]

Thus by 1831 (and compounded by the July Revolution in France) French interests in colonizing Senegal had waned (the new government was unwilling to invest further in the colony) and, with one exception, the commercial life of Senegal for the next twenty-three years was to revert almost entirely to that of the old trading economy. The one exception, however, was to shape the economic fortune of Senegal to the present day; this was the commercial exploitation of the peanut.

The peanut was introduced in West Africa by the Portuguese, who brought it over from South America early in the sixteenth century. It was first grown in Africa as a supplemental subsistence crop along the Guinea and west coasts of West Africa. The first recorded thought given to developing the commercial possibilities of the nut was in 1824, when the Colonial Minister sent a dispatch to Governor Roger advising him that "the peanut should do well in Senegal because it does well in the most arid regions of India." [22] Three years later Interim-Governor Gerbidon, on the basis of studies made at Richard-Toll, sent a memorandum to the minister stating that he recommended "strongly its cultivation, and that it yields an excellent oil." [23] Unfortunately, these studies and results were recorded during the period of French disillusionment with the colony, and nothing further was done at this point to promote its cultivation actively.

Although the French government did little further to create a modern colony out of its holdings in Senegal until the assumption to the governorship by General Louis Faidherbe in 1854 (see Chapter 2), private French merchants and traders (and later the French government) took an interest in the peanut, and small amounts were grown in the lower reaches of the Senegal River and along the "Petite-Côte." In 1834 the Bordeaux trading firm of Devès et Chaumet requested that it be allowed to take over a former indigo mill in Saint Louis for the purpose of setting up a small peanut-oil extraction plant. This request was refused by the colonial government. Six years later a similar request was made by a local merchant, who died before a final decision was made. By this time, however, the French government had once again, though cautiously, turned its attention to Senegal, though not the Senegal of cotton and indigo. The need of French industry for vegetable oils had grown rapidly by 1840, and in that year the Colonial Minister suggested that the colonial government encourage the gathering and planting of such vegetable-oil seeds as argan, sesame, castor seed, and especially the peanut. This the colonial government did, but refused to subsidize the growing of these crops as it had done earlier with the growing of cotton and indigo. Nevertheless, production, notably of the peanut, increased rapidly, although limited largely to regions of easy accessibility, mainly along the coast and in the Senegal River region. By 1847 Governor Protet, taking note of the rapid spread of commercial peanut cultivation, wrote to the Colonial Minister:

The natives are beginning to understand seriously the use that they can make of their land by devoting themselves to the production of a crop which requires little work and fits in with their natural inclination towards laziness. . . . Peanuts will probably save the country.[24]

From 1841 on, the general trend of peanut production in Senegal went up rapidly. Exports increased from 266 tons in 1841 to 3,000 tons in 1853. By 1856 exports increased to almost 6,000 tons; by 1870 the figure reached 8,772 tons; and by 1885 amounted to 45,061 tons. Although the general trend was up, there were (as there are today) fluctuations in production induced by yearly variations in the rainfall pattern, and some now-familiar changes and trends were noted for the first time:

Buying and selling of peanuts became a sort of dangerous game. At about this time some voices were raised denouncing the dangers of monoculture. The Moniteur du Sénégal recorded the complaints of provincial administrators in whose "cercles" famines resulted from the reduction in the planting of subsistence crops. The enormous development of peanut cultivation, at first along the "Petite-Côte," then in the Cayor and Casamance, then in the Djolof, corresponded exactly with the progress of pacification in the countryside.[25]

In 1885 a new and important element was introduced in Senegal to spread commercial peanut cultivation even more rapidly—the railroad.

In that year the Dakar–Saint Louis Railroad was completed. Its completion coupled with the complete pacification of the Cayor a few years later resulted in the development of that region during the end of the nineteenth and the beginning of the twentieth centuries into the principal peanut-producing region of Senegal. In 1896 peanut exports from Senegal reached 65,555 tons; in 1900 more than 140,000 tons were exported; and in 1914 the figure reached 280,000 tons. The economic development of Senegal was now tied firmly to the peanut, the commercial expansion of which was conditioned largely by the construction of the rail web and the pacification of the countryside. As André Villard wrote:

[In the course of our study] we have cited many names and figures, but the most important character by far in the history of Senegal is the peanut. Indeed, towards it go the thoughts of governors anxious with their budgets, those of the farmers anxious of their profits, and towards it the anxiety of all those who sell and buy anything in Senegal. It gives rise to money and manufactured goods. It reigns incontestably over the country . . . and it influences the construction of ports and railroads as well as political decisions. It has contributed to the pacification of the country by attracting and enriching certain peoples who once thought only of war. Its production led to the construction of railroads, and railroads increased its production still further.[26]

The completion of the Thiès-Kayes rail link in 1923 (plus the Guinguinéo-Kaolack and Diourbel-Touba spurs) coupled with the depletion of the soils in the Cayor shifted the main peanut-producing regions of Senegal to the region of the Baol and, to a lesser extent, to the regions of the Rip, Casamance, and the Boundou, the basic pattern that still exists today. With the opening up of this new territory to peanut cultivation plus the setting up of research stations, the general trend of peanut production and exports continued to climb. After a drop during World War I, commercial production stabilized at approximately 400,000 tons annually between 1923 and 1932, increased to 600,000 tons in 1938 and 1939, and dropped sharpiy during World War II. (The disruption of traditional trading patterns caused a decrease in peanut exports to France plus a decrease in rice imports and forced the Senegalese farmer to substitute the growing of millet for peanuts.) By 1957 production had surpassed the 1938 and 1939 figures, with commercial production reaching 984,677 tons during the 1965–1966 peanut year (total Senegalese production, including that auto-consumed, amounted to 1,121,925 tons). Today Senegal ranks among the five leading peanut producing nations of the world and vies with Nigeria as the leading exporter of peanuts and peanut derivatives (see Table 25).

TABLE 25   Principal Peanut-Producing and Exporting Countries for 1965
(1,000 Short Tons of Undecorticated Peanuts or Peanut Equivalent)

Country	Production	%	Export	%
India	4,960	28.6	11.4	0.3
China	2,490	14.4	100.0	2.9
Nigeria	1,700	9.8	1,190.5	34.8
United States	1,252	7.2	220.7	6.4
Senegal	1,195	6.9	832.8	24.3
Brazil	730	4.2	NA	...
Burma	500	2.9	NA	...
Argentina	484	2.8	200.2	5.8
Indonesia	415	2.4	NA	...
Sudan	316[a]	1.8	216.7	6.3
Niger	300	1.7	161.5	4.7
South Africa	219	1.3	53.7	1.6
Uganda	175[a]	1.0	NA	...
Chad	165	1.0	NA	...
Japan	162	0.9	NA	...
Malawi	160	0.9	NA	...
Cameroon	138	0.9	NA	...
Thailand	133	0.8	NA	...
Mali	130	0.7	66.0	1.9
Gambia	112	0.6	96.0	2.8
Mexico	108	0.6	NA	...
Other countries	1,506	8.7	275.5	8.0
Estimated world total	17,350	100.0	3,425.0	100.0

Source: United States Department of Agriculture, Foreign Agricultural Service, *Fats, Oils, and Oil Seeds,* FFO 8–66 (July 1966), pp. 2 and 4.

The principal commercial peanut producing regions of Senegal today are in the southwestern part of the country, in the administrative regions of Kaolack, Diourbel, Thiès, and Casamance (see Table 26). These administrative regions correspond roughly with the historic regions of Cayor, the Baol, Sine-Saloum, the Rip, and Casamance. Until the construction of the Thiès-Kayes link of the Dakar-Niger Railroad (completed in 1923),

TABLE 26 Peanut Production in Senegal for the 1965–1966 Peanut Year by Administrative Regions

(*in metric tons*)

Region	Total Production	%	Commercial Production	%
Kaolack	528,000	47.1	466,047	47.3
Diourbel	264,400	23.6	245,184	24.9
Thiès	142,600	12.7	129,886	13.2
Casamance	132,350	11.8	105,440	10.7
Eastern Senegal (Senegal Oriental)	36,275	3.2	33,158	3.4
River (Fleuve)	15,900	1.4	3,938	0.4
Cape Verde (Cap-Vert)	2,400	0.2	1,024	0.1
Total	1,121,925	100.0	984,677	100.0

Source: Contrôle Financier du Sénégal, *La Campagne Arachidière 1965–1966 au Sénégal*, pp. 3 and 5.

the principal peanut growing regions of Senegal were the Cayor and, to a lesser extent, the "Petite-Côte" and the Senegal River Valley, which were drained by the Dakar–Saint Louis Railroad, the spur between Louga and Linguère, and small evacuation ports along the coast. Inevitably, the intensive and extensive growing of the peanut season after season without fertilization and/or proper rotation practices led by the 1920s to the general depletion of these sandy soils, and today they are (with the exception of the southern portion of the Cayor near Thiès) minor producers of the nut. This shift to the south resulted in a general reorientation of the economic pattern of Senegal. It de-emphasized the importance of the Senegal River region (and Saint Louis, which nevertheless remained the capital of Senegal) and led to the installation of commercial institutions in these newly opened up areas. By 1929 Kaolack was a modern port. With this shift, the present-day evacuation pattern of the peanut started to emerge: instead of moving to overseas markets via Saint Louis, Dakar, and small coastal evacuation points such as Rufisque, M'Bour, Nianing, and others, the peanut now started to drain largely to the two important peanut-evacuation ports of Dakar and Kaolack. (Ziguinchor continued to be the principal drainer of Casamance.)

Today the port of Dakar is virtually the sole drainer of the commer-

FIG. 29   Cultivating peanuts in the Sine-Saloum region of Senegal

cial peanut production of the Diourbel, Thiès, River, and Cape Verde regions, and competes with Kaolack and the other ports of the Saloum Estuary for the output of the regions of Kaolack and Eastern Senegal. For evacuation points in these two regions that lie close to the railroad, the choice between Kaolack and Dakar for the evacuation of decorticated nuts is generally an arbitrary one, since the greater rail haul cost to Dakar is largely obviated by the difficulties of navigation on the Saloum Estuary, the loss of time, and the necessity to complete the loading at Dakar. Since the Cape Verde industrial complex has the largest peanut-oil extraction capacity of Senegal (three of Senegal's six peanut-oil plants are located on the peninsula), an added attraction is furnished for peanut movements in this direction. This industrial function of the Cape Verde region is reflected in the nature of peanut and peanut-derivative embarkations at the port of Dakar. In 1965 while the port accounted for approximately 60 per cent of the total volume of peanut and peanut-derivative embarkations at the ports of Senegal, it accounted for only 50 per

FIG. 30   Stocking peanuts in the Sine-Saloum region of Senegal

cent of the peanut embarkations but for 68 per cent of the peanut-oil and cake loadings (see Table 21).[27]

The historical and current importance of the peanut to the economic development of Senegal (as well as to cargo movements at the port of Dakar) cannot be overemphasized. It was peanut cultivation that changed the entire character of the Senegalese economy from a basically subsistence economy with limited commercial gathering to one in which approximately one-half the cultivated land is devoted to growing one crop, the peanut. Fortunately, the physical base of much of Senegal, with fairly rich, sandy soils and a minimum rainfall of 355 millimeters, lends itself well to the production of this crop (see Chapter 1). Unfortnuately, the sahelian and drier savanna climates that cover most of Senegal largely preclude the growing of most other commerical crops without the development of irrigation works. Only in the valley of the Senegal River is sufficient water available to set up such schemes on a large scale, but until recently there was little incentive (and capital) to consider such programs seriously. The expansion of peanut cultivation to the southern regions of the country was sufficient to attract migrants from the drier north and east (as well as from French Sudan, the Gambia, Portuguese Guinea, and French Guinea), to create a relatively prosperous agricultural class,[28] and to provide adequate revenue (directly and indirectly) for the territory. Consequently, Senegal became a classic example of a monocultural country. Until the postwar period, when a local industry catering to a larger West African market was established and phosphate exports were introduced, peanuts and peanut derivatives accounted for over 90 per cent of the exports of Senegal; today, as was noted earlier, the figure is still high, being approximately 75 per cent. The peanut has brought relative prosperity to a land that 120 years ago was almost abandoned as having no agricultural potential. This relative prosperity, however, is one that has to a very large extent been maintained artificially by the former colonial power.

During the period of peanut expansion in Senegal, the farmer generally had to decide whether to continue the traditional subsistence agriculture (which, owing to the physical nature of the country, was based largely on the growing of millet) or to switch to commercial peanut cultivation. Because the growing season of approximately 120 days (from June to September) is too short for double cropping, the choice was generally one or the other. Since millet yields on the average 300 to 500 kilograms per hectare while peanuts yield 800 to 1,000 kilograms per hectare, the choice, if the farmer was close enough to an evacuation route,[29] was inevitably the peanut. In addition, the peanut had other advantages: it was easily cropped, offered less danger of attacks by parasites and pests, and opened up a new world of material goods to the farmer. Therefore while peanut production went up so did the dependence upon purchased food, for the most part local millet or imported Indochinese rice. Until World War II, however, the price of peanuts in France was conditioned by the commodity markets in Bordeaux and Marseilles, and a drop in prices meant a loss of income to the farmer. If at the same time the price of imported rice from Indochina rose or, as happened in 1940, the supply was cut off, the result was hunger and often famine, and a return to sub-

FIG. 31   A pile of undecorticated peanuts in the Sine-Saloum region of
Senegal, with two decorticating "machines" in the foreground

sistence agriculture. To assist the Senegalese producer and to guarantee
a supply of peanuts during the 1930s and during World War II, two important steps were taken by the French: local decortication of the peanut
was introduced and, during the war, a guaranteed minimum price was set
up for the nut at the ports of France.

Until the 1930s most of the peanuts left Senegal in undecorticated
form. Then, during the cost-cutting depression days, local decortication
was introduced to lower the cost of shipment and thus meet the prevailing low prices; decortication reduces the weight of the nut by 28 to 30
per cent.[30] The decorticating "machine" is a small cage on a horizontal
axis inside of which is a manually operated beater-arm which breaks the
nut and separates the kernel from the shell, the mixture falling through
the bars of the cage (see Fig. 31). The kernel is then separated from the
shell fragments by winnowing. The average "machine" has a daily capacity of 20 to 30 tons of undecorticated peanuts. There are hundreds of
these simple decorticating "machines" scattered throughout the peanut-
producing regions of Senegal, their limited size and simple nature making
them easy to operate. The effect of these "machines" upon the economy

of Senegal has been profound. They helped save much of the Senegalese (as well as French Sudanese) peanut industry during the depression years; they added an additional income earner to the local economy; they provided a new commodity (the shell) for use as a local fuel (the city of Ziguinchor, for example, generates all its electricity by the burning of the peanut shells at the SEIC plant);[31] and, from the specific point of view of this study, they modified greatly (along with oil extraction) the pattern of peanut embarkations at the ports of Senegal (see Table 19). Today virtually no peanuts leave Senegal in the undecorticated state; those that do are used mainly for roasting and for confections.

During World War II, to assure a supply of peanuts in the Metropole, a C.I.F. price for the nut was fixed at the ports of France, from which was determined the price at the ports of Dakar, Kaolack, and Ziguinchor, this in turn determining a set price to be paid to the producers. From this arrangement evolved the system (which was to be terminated after the 1963–1964 peanut year)[32] of preferential quota and price whereby France agreed to take a certain amount of Senegalese peanuts, part of which were to be bought at a certain minimum price. This price was usually well above the open market price. In addition France agreed not to buy peanuts outside the franc zone as long as Senegal could sup-

FIG. 32   The Trans-Gambia Highway, which connects the Port of Dakar with the regions of Sine-Saloum, Rip, and Casamance

ply her needs. Prior to Senegalese independence the quota and price were fixed by decree in Paris; after independence the quota and price were determined by negotiations between France and Senegal. For the 1963–1964 peanut year France agreed to take the equivalent of 215,000 tons of refined peanut oil from Senegal. This quota was to be met by 212,500 tons of decorticated peanuts (set at the equivalent of 97,750 tons of refined oil) at a guaranteed price of 1.05 French francs per kilogram (52,-500 francs CFA per metric ton)[33] C.I.F. at the ports of France and 117,250 tons of refined oil (or the equivalent in unrefined oil) at a price to be agreed upon by the French and Senegalese oil producers. (This price was subsequently set at 95,585 francs CFA per ton of unrefined oil.) The average world market prices during this period were 43,000 francs CFA per ton for decorticated peanuts and 69,250 francs CFA per ton for unrefined peanut oil. Therefore the agreed prices were 9,500 francs CFA (22 per cent) above the average world market price for decorticated peanuts and 26,335 francs CFA (38 per cent) above the average world market price for unrefined peanut oil.[34] Since only 187,700 tons of decorticated peanuts and the equivalent of 124,100 tons of refined oil (set at the equivalent of 129,240 tons of unrefined oil) were sent to France during the 1963–1964 peanut year, the French subsidies for the year amounted to approximately the following:

$$187,700 \times 9,500 \text{ francs CFA} = 1,783,150,000 \text{ francs CFA}$$
$$129,240 \times 26,335 \text{ francs CFA} = 3,403,550,000 \text{ francs CFA}$$

$$\text{Total Subsidy} \qquad 5,186,700,000 \text{ francs CFA}$$
$$\text{or}$$
$$21,170,204 \text{ U.S. dollars}$$

An additional subsidy to Senegalese producers came from the retail sale of peanut oil on the African (notably Senegalese) market. Since these oil prices are determined by the prices set by the French peanut-oil producers, an estimated additional 999,676,600 franc CFA (4,080,313 U.S. dollar) subsidy came from this source.[35]

The future for the Senegalese peanut industry is very problematical. Under the terms of the Convention of Association with the European Economic Community that Senegal signed in July 1963 and which came into force in June 1964, Senegal was to lose all subsidy and quota benefits from France effective November 1, 1964 (subsequently extended by France and Senegal to include the 1965–1966 peanut year), and Senegalese peanut and peanut-oil prices were to adjust themselves to prevailing world market prices. In return the Common Market will allow Senegalese peanuts and peanut derivatives to enter free of duty and quotas; will eventually place a common external tariff on imported vegetable oils and oil seeds from non-associate states; and will, over a five-year period (starting in 1965), extend to Senegal a grant of 11.6 billion francs CFA (47.3 million U.S. dollars) to cushion the loss of the French subsidies. This Common Market grant is to be used as follows: 75 per cent to improve peanut production and marketing methods (the use of fertilizer and farm machinery, seed selection, rural education, organization of cooperatives, improvement of storage facilities, etc.) and 25 per cent to aid in the diversification of Senegalese agriculture (to develop more intensively other commercial agriculture and to encourage the planting of food crops). It is hoped that over the five-year transition period (after which this aid from the Common Market will end) Senegalese peanut production will increase by approximately 5 per cent annually, so that by the end of 1969 commercial peanut production will be over 1,000,000 tons annually and that the peanut farmer's decrease of income per kilogram will be wiped out by an increase in his volume of production as well as by improved marketing operations. In addition, an increase in the domestic production of other crops such as cotton, rice, millet, sugar cane, and sisal will reduce Senegal's present-day large dependence for these commodities on extra-Senegalese sources. Emphasis will also be placed upon international cooperation to stabilize world prices of primary products, notably oils and oil seeds, through such institutions as the General Agreement on Tariffs and Trade (GATT), the United Nations, and the new African Peanut Council (le Conseil Africain de l'Arachide), whose members are Senegal, Nigeria, Niger, and Upper Volta.

There is little doubt that peanut and other agricultural production in Senegal can be increased substantially in the near future. Although it is true that much of Senegal is basically unsuited for agriculture (the vast Ferlo Plateau of central Senegal is generally too arid, has a low water table, and has no permanent streams), much of Senegal can be farmed more intensively. In the past the practice of monoculture led to the growing of one crop on the same land year after year without proper crop rotation and soil management on much of the land in Senegal. In addition, much of the vegetation was cut down indiscriminately as peanut culture spread. The result was soil depletion and erosion. This problem is most severe in the early peanut lands of the Cayor and near Linguère, which at one time were the leading peanut-producing regions of Senegal but today are regions of depleted soils and poor agriculture. Another problem is that most of the tribes that practice sedentary argiculture, such as the Wolof, do not raise animals (or send them away for grazing) and thus lose the advantages of natural fertilization, while those that practice animal husbandry, such as the Peul (or Fulani), do not engage in sedentary agriculture. Only the Serers of the regions of Thiès and Kaolack practice this type of mixed agriculture with excellent results. Thus an intensive effort in the coming years in the fields of soil erosion prevention, crop rotation, the use of manure and fertilizer (the natural phosphates near Thiès can and will be used for fertilizer production), and seed selection should lead to an increase in peanut production in the coming years. If the Senegalese development plans are fulfilled, the average peanut yield per hectare will increase from 1,007 kilograms (which is what it was during the 1965–1966 peanut year) to 1,125 kilograms by 1969,[36] and total production will be over 1,000,000 tons annually (barring any natural calamity, such as the dry summer of 1966).

An important step in increasing the efficiency of peanut marketing was taken in 1960 when legislation was passed to encourage the development of agricultural cooperatives and the Office de Commercialisation Agricole (OCA) was set up. This is a state trading agency which has a monopoly in the buying of the commercial peanut crop from the cooperatives and from individual farmers and controls the supplies of peanuts to the oil mills as well as for export. Until the 1960–1961 peanut season all the commercial peanut crop in Senegal was produced by individual farmers and sold entirely to the large trading firms (such as the Compagnie Française de l'Afrique Occidentale, the Société Commerciale de l'Ouest Africain, and the Nouvelle Société Commerciale Africaine), either directly through their agents or indirectly through private intermediaries, mainly Lebanese. Often there was another intermediary, usually an African, between the agent or the private intermediary and the grower. After the usual advances and loans (and high interest rates) to the grower, he would usually get approximately 30 per cent less than the official price. Today all the commercial peanut crop is bought by OCA, either directly through field stations or from "organismes stockeurs." These are licensed, responsible individuals or firms that operate on set margins. Yet even these will be eliminated eventually as more OCA field stations are set up.

In addition the cooperatives have taken away many of the former functions of the private middlemen by making loans and advances to their members, selling supplies at cost, and assisting in the marketing of the peanut crop to OCA. Since their creation in 1960, the cooperatives have been marketing a larger percentage of the peanut crop each year, accounting for 72 per cent of the commercialized crop during the 1965–1966 peanut season. Therefore since 1960 the Senegalese government has consciously attempted to squeeze out the profit-sharing middlemen by taking over the marketing of the peanut through its agency, OCA, and by encouraging the setting up of cooperatives. It is perhaps too early to judge the full success of this program, but it is a big step in meeting the challenge posed by the removal of the French subsidies.

As well as improving production and marketing methods, Senegal has taken a third important step, the diversification of agriculture, to soften the impact of the loss of French subsidies and the subjection of Senegalese peanut prices to the fluctuations of world oil and oilseed prices. Over the past one hundred years, as Senegal went from a subsistence economy to a commercial, largely monocultural economy, the country became more and more dependent upon imported foodstuffs. In 1965 Senegal imported 179,221 tons of rice, 66,072 tons of sugar, 53,471 tons of fruits and vegetables, 16,615 tons of corn, and many other agricultural commodities that very probably could be grown economically in the country if proper steps, such as irrigation, were taken. Today plans are underway to increase local production of many of these crops. While development plans call for continued emphasis on and intensification of peanut cultivation in the "basin arachidier"—that is, the regions of Kaolack, Diourbel, and Thiès—plans also call for the expansion of subsidiary crop production elsewhere, notably in the Senegal River Valley and in Casamance. It is important to note that, with the exception of the increase in commercial peanut production, agricultural development plans for Senegal do not call for the creation of new export agricultural schemes but for the increase of domestic production of food staples to keep down imports and thus to make the country more self-sufficient and less vulnerable to possible future fluctuations in world oil and oilseed prices. The greatest effort in agricultural diversification is being expended in the Senegal River region, where numerous government and private organizations operating out of Richard-Toll are in the process of studying the feasibility of such schemes. The principal organizations and their areas of interests are:

1. Institut de Recherches Agronomiques Tropicales et des Cultures Vivrières (IRAT) research station—irrigated rice, irrigated sugar cane, cereals, and miscellaneous industrial crops;

2. Compagnie Française des Textiles Tropicaux (CFDT) experimental station—irrigated cotton;

3. Centre de Multiplication de Semences—irrigated rice;

4. Office de la Recherche Scientifique et Technique Outre-Mer (ORSTOM) research station—ornithological studies; and

5. Société de Développement Rizicole du Sénégal (SDRS)—irrigated rice and cotton (took over the operation of the Delta Irrigation Scheme in 1960).

Despite problems of soil salinity, incursions of sea water during the dry season, and costs, the various organizations are generally optimistic about the potentialities of the Senegal River region.[37] In addition to the operations of SDRS, which has over 5,000 hectares under cultivation with an annual yield of 13,000 to 16,000 tons of rice, operations are underway to develop an additional 30,000 hectares of rice land in the delta region. When completed in stages over an estimated ten-year period at a total cost of approximately 4.5 billion francs CFA (18.4 million U.S. dollars), this new scheme is expected to yield approximately 60,000 tons of rice annually. Attempts to grow sugar cane have also been successful, and studies are currently underway to find suitable land for its cultivation; it is felt that 14,000 hectares will be sufficient to satisfy the present-day needs of Senegal. If further studies prove successful, this region may also become a supplier of fruits (mangoes, bananas, grapefruit, oranges, and dates), sisal, cotton, and other commercial crops. In Casamance, already the principal rice-producing region of Senegal, plans have been advanced to increase this production by draining the mangrove swamps and planting more upland areas to this crop. In addition, because of the modified Guinean climate of Casamance, plans have been made to expand the output of fruits and vegetables, oil palm, and coconut palm.

Thus from the specific point of view of our study (and assuming the fulfillment of the plans), while peanut and peanut-derivative embarkations at the port of Dakar will probably increase in the future, debarkations of certain imported food and other staples should decrease as domestic production increases. Another factor that will tend to lower such debarkations at the port of Dakar is the reopening of the former Dakar-Niger Railroad between Senegal and Mali and the importation of rice and cotton from Mali, chiefly from the Office du Niger. During the 1964–1965 fiscal year of the Régie des Chemins de Fer du Sénégal (the Senegal Railroad), an estimated 13,000 tons (10,000 tons of rice and millet and 3,000 tons of cotton) of such staples were expected to move from Mali to Dakar.[38]

Assuming that Senegal can generally make the above adjustments, the big remaining problem is whether or not markets can be found for the increased peanut production (production is planned to increase by 35 to 40 per cent between 1964 and 1969). In the past, as was noted earlier, virtually all the peanut and peanut-derivative exports have gone to France owing to the subsidized market. Although this subsidization will no longer exist, Senegal's association with the Common Market will give it certain tariff preferences. Consequently most of the increased production should move to this market if a place can be found for it. In a study prepared in 1963 by Christian Valantin, the director of OCA, it was shown that the Common Market countries had a combined market of approximately 2,600,000 tons of vegetable oil (oil equivalent). Of this total, only 18 per cent (460,000 tons) was supplied by the Common Market countries (mainly rape and olive oils).[39] The rest was imported from outside. Thus association with the Common Market will give Senegal (as well as the other associate members) a preference in supplying this deficit.

An examination of the nature of the vegetable-oil imports into the Common Market shows another favorable factor. The bulk of the edible oils and oilseeds imported into the Common Market are middle latitude oils and seeds (such as soybean and rapeseed) coming from non-associate members, mainly the United States (see Table 27). The tariff preference given to Senegal and other associate members should allow them to compete effectively for this market. In addition, the long association (and in some cases, direct control) between oil producers and peanut sellers in Senegal and purchasers in France assures a subjective preference to the Senegalese products in France, which is the leading peanut-oil consuming country in the world. (There is a strong preference for peanut oil in France, where it accounts for most of the edible oil consumption, mainly as salad and cooking oil with a small amount used for making margarine.) Although Nigeria's association with the Common Market (effective in 1966) coupled with the expansion of peanut cultivation in the region of Maiduguri will dilute somewhat an otherwise extremely favorable position for Senegal, there are some safeguards. As was noted earlier, Nigerian oil imports by the Common Market will be subject to a quota until 1969, traditional Nigerian markets (notably the United Kingdom) must be served, and the fact that French peanut requirements normally were not met by the states of the Community (in 1965 France was Nigeria's largest customer for decorticated peanuts) bodes well for the Senegalese peanut industry. If Senegal can meet her growth plans, there is little doubt that under present conditions markets can be found for her peanut and peanut-oil exports.

Agricultural exports other than peanuts play a very minor role in the export economy of Senegal and consequently in the cargo-embarkation pattern of the port of Dakar. In 1965 the three principal non-peanut agricultural exports were palm kernels (3,757 tons), gum arabic (2,216 tons), and hides and skins (1,196 tons). Collectively they amounted to 0.5 and 1.5, respectively, of the volume and value of Senegalese exports for that year. Since virtually all the oil palm grows in the modified Guinean climatic zone of Casamance, no palm kernel embarkations were recorded at the port of Dakar in 1963; they were all exported via the port of Ziguinchor. Although plans for future development call for the expansion of this culture, this will take place in Casamance and will not affect cargo movements at Dakar. Exports of hides and skins should also increase in the future.

TABLE 27   Gross Imports of Vegetable Oils and Oil Seeds into the European Economic Community for 1961

(In Thousands of Tons)

	West Germany	France	Nether-lands	Italy	Belgium– Luxembourg
Peanuts					
Seed	80	486	44	72	59
Oil	18	106	6	. . .	4
Soybean					
Seed	892	80	259	201	89
Oil	11	1	6	10	1
Cottonseed					
Seed	1	. . .	. . .	. . .	. . .
Oil	72	. . .	1	. . .	4
Rapeseed					
Seed	25	32	3	64	2
Oil	5	. . .	3	1	. . .
Other edible seeds					
Seed	23	1	2	111	6
Oil	45	24	11	100	2
Copra					
Seed	265	88	157	19	36
Oil	36	1	2	19	4
Palm kernels					
Seed	126	81	141	. . .	23
Oil	11	1	. . .	9	2
Palm oil					
Seed	. . .	. . .	. . .	. . .	. . .
Oil	76	31	88	24	42
Linseed					
Seed	10	78	91	13	28
Oil	80	21	4	16	. . .
Other					
Seed	22	10	3	9	3
Oil	7	28	2	2	1
All oils and oil seeds (1,000 tons oil equiv.)	807	584	387	322	150

Source: Commonwealth Economic Committee, *Vegetable Oils and Oilseeds* (London: H.M.S.O., 1962), p. 220.

In the past, animal husbandry by the peoples of Senegal, with the exception of the Peuls and the Serers, was subordinate to the raising of subsistence crops or, more recently, the peanut. For the Peuls animal husbandry is an end in itself—a sign of dignity and wealth—and the cattle are not raised for commercial sale. Therefore only the Serers of the Kaolack, Diourbel, and Thiès regions have contributed significantly to the commercial raising of cattle, mainly zebus. Development plans call for the encouragement of this largely neglected activity (for hides, meat, and manure) by establishing cooperatives of herders, setting up rural slaughterhouses, developing pastures, and by controlled breeding. The bulk of the increased exports will probably pass through the port of Dakar. Much of the gum arabic passing through Dakar is traditionally from Mauritania, with some coming from Mali. In 1965 port statistics recorded 4,724 tons as having been loaded, with Senegalese export statistics for that year indicating that Senegal provided 47 per cent of these embarkations. With the construction of the new port at Port Étienne, the wharf at Nouakchott, and the development of feeder roads in Mauritania, most of the Mauritanian trade will probably be lost by Dakar. Only the limited outputs of Senegal and Mali will probably continue to drain to the

FIG. 33   Zebu cattle, one of the principle exports of Mali

port. There are no plans to encourage actively an expansion in this production. Since most of the emphasis in future non-peanut agricultural expansion will be placed on the development of staples for local Senegalese consumption, agricultural commodities other than peanuts will play a very minor role in the future export pattern of Senegal. The development, on the other hand, of agricultural schemes in the Senegal River Valley and its delta and in Casamance could lead to an increase in cabotage movements between Ziguinchor and a rejuvenated Saint Louis and other Senegal River ports.

In 1965 minerals accounted for 67 per cent of the total volume of cargo embarkations at the port of Dakar (see Table 13), and for 58.5 per cent and 8.6 per cent, respectively, of the total volume and value of Senegalese exports (see Table 24). The two minerals that contributed to these statistics are phosphates and salt. The most important of these by far in terms of present-day port and foreign-trade statistics and future importance are the phosphate deposits near Thiès. In 1965 phosphates alone accounted for 99 per cent of the total volume of mineral embarkations at the port of Dakar and for virtually all of Senegal's mineral exports (see Table 24). The first phosphate operations in Senegal were started in 1948 by the Compagnie de Produits Chimiques et Électromagnétiques Péchiney, which became the Société Sénégalaise des Phosphates de Thiès after Senegal became independent in 1960. It is a subsidiary of the famous Société des Produits Chimiques Péchiney-Saint-Gobain. Using open-pit methods, this company mines aluminum phosphate deposits at Pallo (an estimated reserve of 100 million tons of phosphate rock with an average concentration of 29.5 per cent P_2O_5), screens it at the mining site, and sends it 10 kilometers by truck to Lam-Lam (on the Dakar-Saint Louis rail line), where it is crushed, screened, and stocked. Some (approximately one-third) is also roasted. Most of this is then sent by rail to Dakar, where it is stored at the Société Sénégalaise des Phosphates de Thiès phosphate quay in the Northwest Zone of the port (see Fig. 22) until it is shipped out. In 1965, although production amounted to approximately 140,000 tons, aluminum phosphates accounted for 111,182 tons (7.5 per cent) of cargo embarkations at the port of Dakar, virtually all of which went to France. At Lam-Lam some phosphate is also baked and pulverized into fertilizer and animal supplement for local use (6,385 tons in 1965, though usually close to 9,000 tons). Although these operations have an annual capacity of 200,000 tons of rock, present-day operations are running at slightly over one-half of this capacity and increasing slowly, the quality of the rock limiting its markets. In the foreseeable future, production will probably not increase significantly, and annual aluminum phosphate embarkations at the port of Dakar will probably continue to be close to 100,000 tons.

In 1957 the Compagnie Sénégalaise des Phosphates de Taïba (TAIBA) was organized to exploit the calcium phosphate deposits at Taïba, 40 kilometers north of Thiès. (Among the participants in this

TABLE 28   World Production of Phosphate Rock for 1965
(*In 1,000 Long Tons*)

Country	Total	%
United States	26,440	40.9
U.S.S.R.	15,260[a]	23.6
Morocco	9,669	15.0
Tunisia	2,992	4.6
Naurau Island	1,472	2.3
North Vietnam	1,029[a]	1.6
Senegal	987	1.5
Togo	958	1.5
China	900[a]	1.4
Jordan	815	1.3
Christmas Island (Indian Ocean)	740	1.1
South Africa	600	0.9
United Arab Republic	584	0.9
Israel	382	0.6
Ocean Island	369	0.6
French Oceania (Makatea Island)	314	0.5
Brazil	259[a]	0.4
North Korea	200[a]	0.3
Peru	166	0.3
Netherlands Antilles	110[a]	0.2
Other Countries	354	0.5
Estimated world total	64,600	100.0

[a] Estimated

Source: United States Department of the Interior, *Phosphate Rock*, Reprint from the Bureau of Mines Minerals Yearbook, prepared by Richard W. Lewis (Washington, 1966), p. 13.

project is an American firm, International Minerals and Chemical Corporation.) Taking into consideration future world demand and operating costs, present reserves are estimated at 75 million tons of rock enriched to a concentration of 82 to 83 per cent tricalcium phosphate. The open-pit operations were started in March 1960, with output reaching 867,000 tons of enriched rock in 1965. The rock is mined, crushed and screened, and, because the grade of the rock as mined is generally uneven and poor, sent to the flotation plant where it is enriched to the 82 to 83 per cent level. It is then dried and stocked. All of these operations take place at Taïba. This enriched rock is then sent by rail (the company has a private rail line joining the main Dakar-Saint Louis line at Tivaouane) to its warehouse (capacity 70,000 tons) on the Northwest Terreplein in the Northwest Zone of the port of Dakar where it is stored until it leaves for world markets. In 1965 calcium phosphate accounted for 873,762 tons (59 per cent) of the volume of cargo embarkations at the port of Dakar. In that same year, markets for this phosphate were found in eight different countries, the principal buyers being, in order, West Germany, Japan, the United Kingdom, and South Africa. This enriched rock is of excellent quality and in high demand on world markets, and the company sees no difficulty in marketing future output (if present market conditions continue), which was expected to reach more than one million tons in 1966.[40]

An additional expansion program already underway calls for the construction of a superphosphate ammonia fertilizer plant by the Société Industrielle d'Engrais au Sénégal (SIES), which is a joint public-private enterprise in which TAIBA is participating. When completed in 1968, it will have an initial capacity of 60,000 tons of fertilizer (eventual capacity 130,000 tons), approximately 10,000 tons of which will probably be exported to other African markets.[41]

Thus the phosphate operations have in recent years become an important contributor to port cargo loadings. With their close proximity to the port of Dakar plus the good railroad connections, they are firmly within the pull of the port. Recent geologic studies have, however, turned up additional large deposits near Louga, Saint Louis, and in the Senegal River Valley near Matam.[42] Should these new deposits prove economically workable, they would, along with the agricultural development schemes of the valley region, be an added incentive for the improvement of transportation on the Senegal River and the rejuvenation of the port of Saint Louis. In any event phosphates will, in the indefinite future, continue to play a very important role in the cargo-loading pattern at the port of Dakar, with total embarkations very probably reaching well over one million tons by 1970.

The second most important mineral contributor to cargo loadings at the port of Dakar is salt. In 1965 salt embarkations at the port amounted to 10,652 tons, or 0.7 per cent of total cargo loadings. Virtually all this total was salt from the marine-salt evaporation works belonging to the Société des Salins du Sine-Saloum on the Saloum Estuary across from the port of Kaolack. The works were founded in 1915 to serve markets in Senegal and French Sudan, and sales soon expanded to include most of French West and Equatorial Africa, Cameroon, Togo, and other states of West Africa. Since independence, however, annual production and sales have decreased (from over 70,000 tons in 1959 to 50,895 tons in 1965) as competitive industries have captured some of its traditional markets. Most of the salt leaves directly from the company's wharf at the site of production, but some is sent to Dakar by truck for transshipment. As long as maritime navigation on the Saloum Estuary exists, most of this low-value, high-volume commodity will continue to move directly to markets via the company's wharf. Should such navigation on the Saloum Estuary be suspended in the future (which would very probably happen if Senegal and the Gambia were to unite and the political and economic barriers to the use of the port of Bathurst were removed), much of this trade would probably move to the port of Dakar. Although Bathurst is slightly closer to Kaolack, the existence of the fine Trans-Gambia Highway plus the fact that the port of Bathurst lies on the south side of the Gambia Estuary would very probably direct much of this trade to Dakar. Thus the future could witness an increase of salt movements at the port of Dakar to over 50,000 tons annually.

Until 1964 the third mineral contributor to Senegalese export statistics was the titanium (ilmenite and rutile) and zirconium (zircon) ores worked by the Société Minière Gaziello et Compagnie, a subsidiary of Péchiney-Saint-Gobain and the Fabriques de Produits Chimiques de Thann et Mulhouse. Founded in 1922, this company extracted until

1963 ilmenite, rutile, and zircon from the beach sands (heavy sands) found along the "Petite-Côte" and on the Sangomar Peninsula near the mouth of the Saloum Estuary. Until 1963 the activities of this company were restricted to the eastern side of Sangomar Peninsula near the village of Djifère, where the sands were dug, enriched, and exported (almost entirely to France) from the company's wharf. With the exhaustion of these deposits in 1963 coupled with the difficulties of navigation on the Saloum Estuary, emphasis was to have been shifted to the beach sands along the "Petite-Côte" between M'Bour and Joal, where a new concentrator and wharf were to have been built at Nianing. However, owing to a drop in world market prices for these ores because of increased output in Malaysia and Australia, where these metals are often a secondary product obtained after the first metal (such as tin) is recovered, it was decided in 1964 to liquidate this company. The last shipment of these ores was made in September 1964, and it appears very unlikely that these mineral exports will resume in the foreseeable future.

Existing geological knowledge of Senegal gives little hope for additional mineral exports other than phosphates, salt, and the titanium and zirconium ores. Although approximately 70 per cent of Senegal lies in a sedimentary basin which geologically has petroleum potential, prospection since 1952 by the Société Africaine des Pétroles (SAP), the Société des Pétroles du Sénégal (SPS), and the Compagnie Française des Pétroles has met with little success. Deposits of hematite and magnetite, spodumene (a lithium mineral), bauxite, chromite, and copper-bearing minerals have been found, but not yet in sufficient quantities to merit serious consideration of economic exploitation. Therefore mineral development in Senegal for the immediate future appears to be limited to phosphates, salt, and limestone (near Rufisque), with virtually all the phosphates and some of the limestone (in the form of cement) and salt moving out through the port of Dakar. As is also generally true for the industries of the Cape Verde industrial complex, independence has had little effect upon the export movement of those minerals depending upon an extra-African (mainly European) market (phosphates), while the one depending upon an intra-African market (salt) has suffered somewhat from African competition. In the foreseeable future cargo-embarkation pattern at the port of Dakar, one can say with a fair degree of certainty that phosphates will continue to be by far the most important mineral as well as the single most important commodity in terms of the volume of port cargo loadings.

Thus the importance of the extra-Cape Verde Senegalese hinterland in the cargo-embarkation pattern of the port of Dakar can largely be measured in terms of two commodities: peanuts and phosphates. Together they accounted for 71 per cent (peanuts for 24 per cent and phosphates for 67 per cent) of the total volume of cargo embarkations at the port in 1965. The relative and absolute importance of each has changed considerably since the prewar years. In 1938, the last full year of peace prior to World War II, peanuts and peanut derivatives accounted for approximately 90 per cent (slightly less than 400,000 tons) of the volume of cargo embarkations at the port, while no phosphates were exported. Twenty years later, with the growth of industries on Cape Verde Peninsula, the development of the aluminum phosphate deposits at Thiès, and the advent of peanut decortication, peanut and peanut-derivative exports accounted for 51 per cent of the volume of cargo loadings and aluminum phosphates for 14 per cent. In 1965, with the development of the Taïba phosphate deposits, peanut and peanut-derivative embarkations accounted for 24 per cent of the total volume of cargo loadings and phosphates for 67 per cent. While independence has had little or no effect upon the peanut and phosphate exports of Senegal (since their markets are almost entirely extra-African), the loss of many of the extra-Senegalese African markets for some of the industries of Cape Verde (plus the increase in output of peanuts and phosphates) has had the effect of increasing the relative importance of peanuts, peanut derivatives, and phosphates in the cargo-loading pattern at Dakar in the post-independence period. In the future it is very likely that phosphate loadings will increase absolutely and relatively (if the 1,200,000-ton output goal for 1970 is met by TAIBA), that peanut and peanut-derivative loadings will increase absolutely (if the 1,000,000-ton goal for commercialized undecorticated peanuts for 1969 is met), and that the importance of the Cape Verde industrial complex will decrease relatively and absolutely unless a true West African customs union is created. It is very unlikely that the Senegalese export mix will, at least under present development plans, vary considerably in substance in the future. The details will change, but peanuts, peanut derivatives and phosphates will very probably continue to be by far the principal exports of Senegal and the principal cargo embarkations at the port of Dakar.

The Malian Hinterland

Prior to the rupture of the Mali Federation in August 1960, virtually all the overseas trade of former French Sudan (now Mali) passed through the Senegalese ports of Dakar and Kaolack. This was not so much the result of geographic necessity as of human inducement, the penetration by the French of the Sudanese interior of West Africa from the west coast of West Africa leading to the early development of transportation lines running in an east-west direction (see Chapter 2). The construction of the Dakar-Niger Railroad from Dakar to Bamako (and Koulikoro) early in the twentieth century consolidated this historic pattern, with the result that by 1960 former French Sudan was firmly tied to Dakar and Kaolack for most of its overseas trade. The creation of the Mali Federation in 1959 further reinforced this colonially induced relationship. The principal line of communication was the Niger River, which is navigable between Koulikoro and Ansongo, and the Dakar-Niger Railroad between Dakar and Koulikoro with an embranchment to Kaolack. Within the territory the principal feeder roads largely led to this great artery. Only the southern regions of the country around the provincial towns of Sikasso, Bougouni, Koutiala, and San escaped the full pull of the Niger River–Dakar-Niger Railroad artery and fell partially within the pull of the Abidjan-Niger Railroad. The economic heartland, however, of former French Sudan (as of present-day Mali) extended from Kayes in the west to Ségou in the east in a long belt roughly paralleling the railroad and river to approximately 50 kilometers on either side of the axis. It was this route that enabled commercial agriculture (chiefly the growing of peanuts) to develop in this territory. In 1959 total recorded exports from former French Sudan amounted to 49,974 tons, of which 47,167 tons (94 per cent) consisted of peanut and peanut derivatives (see Table 29).[43] Of this total, approximately 86 per cent moved on the Dakar-Niger Railroad; an additional 3 per cent moved down the Senegal River from the river port of Kayes, while an

TABLE 29   Recorded Exports of (French) Sudan for 1959 and Mali for 1965
(*In Metric Tons*)

Commodity	1959 Volume	%	1965 Volume	%
Decorticated peanuts	38,133	76.3	22,198	33.5
Undecorticated peanuts	25	0.1	. . .	. . .
Peanut oil	9,009	18.0	. . .	. . .
Peanut cake	. . .	. . .	3,054	4.6
Live animals	5	. . .	11,064	16.7
Cotton	. . .	. . .	8,523	12.8
Cotton seed	. . .	. . .	7,014	10.6
Salted, dried, and smoked fish	. . .	. . .	6,837	10.3
Petroleum products	. . .	. . .	1,731	2.6
Salt	. . .	. . .	1,110	1.7
Sesame seed	. . .	. . .	500	0.8
Meat	25	0.1	398	0.6
Hides and skins	1,144	2.3	333	0.5
Shea butter	36	0.1	263	0.4
Gum arabic	1,234	2.5	165	0.2
Wool	147	0.3	116	0.2
Kapok	177	0.4	7	. . .
Beeswax	34	0.1	6	. . .
Millet and sorghum	. . .	. . .	6	. . .
Rice	. . .	. . .	1	. . .
Other	5	. . .	3,034	4.6
Total	49,974	100.0	66,360	100.0

Sources: (*a*) "La République du Mali," *Notes et Études Documentaires*, No. 2,739 (13 Janvier 1961), p. 38; and (*b*) République du Mali, Ministère d'État Chargé du Plan et de la Coordination des Affaires Économiques et Financières, Service de la Statistique Générale et de la Comptabilité Économique Nationale, *Statistiques du Commerce Extérieur* (*Commerce Spécial*) *1965*.

estimated 7 per cent moved toward the Gulf of Guinea. The remaining 4 per cent (chiefly skins, fruits, vegetables, and meat) moved out by air.[44] Although import statistics are not available, in-movements from Senegal on the Dakar-Niger Railroad amounted to 167,000 tons. Much of this freight, however, consisted of cement and other products of the Cape Verde industrial complex and local movement of other commodities; imports from overseas amounted to considerably less than this amount. Since the port of Kaolack accounted for approximately 20,000 tons of its exports and approximately 15,000 tons of its imports, former

French Sudan (present-day Mali) probably accounted for approximately 100,000 tons (less than 10 per cent) of cargo handlings at the port of Dakar in 1959, the last full year before the rupture of the Dakar-Niger Railroad.

Between August 1960 and July 1963 trade and political relations between Senegal and newly created Mali were severed, and alternate overseas trade routes had to be developed. During this period over 85 per cent of the overseas trade of Mali passed via the Abidjan-Niger Railroad and the port of Abidjan; most of the remainder moved through the ports of Conakry and, to a much lesser extent, Cotonou.[45] Despite the fact that during this 34-month period the road network between Mali and Upper Volta and the Ivory Coast was greatly improved (see Chapter 5), when the railroad between Mali and Senegal was reopened the overseas-trade pattern of Mali largely reverted to the colonially induced pattern, and today most of the overseas trade of Mali moves once again through Senegal. The factors of tradition plus economics dictated a return to the old system. Two new important elements have been introduced, however: (1) Mali, no longer wishing to be virtually entirely dependent upon a single extranational overseas outlet, has maintained close commercial ties with Upper Volta and the Ivory Coast (approximately 40,000 tons of cargo that formerly would have moved through the ports of Senegal have been lost to the port of Abidjan)[46] and has kept open indefinite plans for the development of links with the Conakry-Niger Railroad and the port of Conakry; and (2) most of Mali's overseas trade passing through Senegal now moves through the Mali free-trade zone on Pier III in the South Zone of the port of Dakar, with almost none moving through the port of Kaolack. It is estimated that during the 1964–1965 fiscal year of the Régie des Chemins de Fer du Sénégal (the Senegal Railroad), approximately 100,000 tons of Malian cargo were to be loaded and unloaded at the port of Dakar.[47] Therefore the total volume of Malian cargo passing through the port today is approximately what it was before independence. The big changes, however, are in the diversion of approximately 40,000 tons of overseas trade to the port of Abidjan and the virtual discontinuance of the use of the port of Kaolack.

It is not likely that overseas exports from Mali will increase substantially in the immediate future. Owing to Mali's landlocked location in the heart of West Africa, the cost of transportation adds an often insurmountable handicap to many of the country's potential exports. This problem is especially acute when one notes that the principal overseas export is the low-value, high-volume peanut. Although the government is not anxious to de-emphasize the importance of this commodity in its economic planning (development plans did call for an increase in its production from 125,000 tons of undecorticated nut in 1959 to 200,000 tons in 1965,[48] a plan not fulfilled), the main emphasis of the government is upon rural agricultural development—that is, upon an increase in the production of and efficiency in the raising of the traditional subsistence crops of Mali (millet, sorghum, rice, and other minor crops), commercial crops for local or intra-West African consumption, fish in the Inland Delta region of the Niger Valley, and livestock. The surplus production of these commodities is traditionally exported to neighboring African states, notably those to the south where there is a climatic complement to the desert, sahelian, and savanna climates of Mali. To achieve these goals, the government has set up village cooperatives, state marketing boards, government technical assistance programs, and agricultural experimental stations, all coming under the general supervision of the Institut de l'Économie Rurale.

In addition, industrial development plans generally call for the development of industries to process local agricultural commodities for domestic consumption and thus cut down on costly import. These include a sugar refinery to process local sugar, cotton gins and a textile complex to process local cotton, a cement factory, modern slaughterhouses, oil-extraction plants to process peanuts, cottonseed, and shea nuts, soap factories, and miscellaneous consumer industries such as fruit-juice canning, vegetable processing, cigarette making, brick yards, and furniture factories.[49] Thus the immediate economic development plans of Mali call for the rationalization of her economy in accordance with her geographic limitations, a factor which will not lead to a marked increase in the volume of overseas exports in the immediate future.

The principal overseas-export crop of Mali is (and will very probably continue to be) the peanut. In terms of production statistics, it is the fourth most important crop in the country, coming behind the important subsistence crops of millet (and sorghum), manioc, and rice. As in Senegal, it does best in the fairly rich, sandy soils of the wetter sahelian and savanna zones. The factor of transportation, however, largely limits commercial peanut cultivation to a narrow zone within 50 kilometers of the axis formed by the Niger River and the Mali Railroad extending from Ségou to Kayes (see Fig. 28). In 1964 a total of 72,130 tons of undecorticated peanuts were commercialized in Mali, with most of this coming from the "cercles" between Ségou and Kayes, inclusive:

(a) Kita, with 24 per cent of the commercialized crop;
(b) Ségou, with 18 per cent;
(c) Bamako, with 12 per cent;
(d) Banamba, with 10 per cent;
(e) Kolokani, with 9 per cent;
(f) Bafoulabé, with 6 per cent; and
(g) Dioïla with 3 per cent.[50]

The peanuts are marketed through the village cooperatives and the state marketing boards. In the peanut belt extending along the railroad from Koulikoro to Kayes, the overseas-evacuation pattern is a simple one. Since the peanuts are harvested and marketed during the dry season, they are hauled by truck from the gathering and marketing centers (where they are first decorticated) directly to stations along the Mali Railroad. East of Koulikoro (and especially in the region of Ségou) the evacuation pattern is more complicated. Since it costs 700 to 1,000 Malian francs less to ship one ton of peanuts from Ségou to Koulikoro by boat than by road,[51] the shipment of most of the peanuts from this region to the railroad is held up until mid-June, when the annual navigation season on the river resumes (see *infra.,* Chapter 5). During the 1964–65 fiscal year of the Senegal Railroad, 16,689 tons of decorticated peanuts moved from Mali to Dakar.[52] An additional 5,000 tons probably also moved from the regions of San, Sikasso, Bougouni, and Koutiala to the Abidjan-Niger Railroad and the port of Abidjan. In the foreseeable future it is not likely that the volume of commercialized decorticated peanuts moving out of Mali to the port of Dakar will increase substantially. Although, as has been noted earlier, agricultural development plans call for an increase in peanut production, much of this increase is for domestic consumption, either as a supplemental food crop or for local processing into peanut oil.

Other overseas agricultural exports of Mali for the immediate and foreseeable future appear to be limited largely to the traditional gathering crops of shea nuts, kapok, gum arabic, and hides and skins. Approximately 4,000 to 5,000 tons of shea nuts are commercialized annually, mainly from the "cercles" of Bamako, Ségou, San, and Koutiala. Most of this production is sent to neighboring countries (chiefly the Ivory Coast and Upper Volta) for processing into shea butter, with overseas exports amounting to less than 1,000 tons. Annual commercial kapok production amounts to approximately 400 tons (from the "cercles" of Bamako, Sikasso, and San), with most of it moving to the Abidjan-Niger Railroad and the port of Abidjan. Gum arabic production totals less than 1,000 tons annually (chiefly from the "cercles" of Timbuktu, Nioro, and Kayes) and moves out over the former Dakar-Niger Railroad. Exports of hides and skins normally amount to approximately 1,300 tons annually, most of which normally move out to Dakar.[53] Thus the volume of overseas agricultural exports from Mali is not high (approximately 25,000 to 50,000 tons) and future prospects not bright, the transportation cost element being the chief limiting factor.

The present-day commercial agricultural significance of Mali is not so much that of a supplier of agricultural commodities for extra-African markets but that of a supplier for other West African states, notably those to the south. In terms of value of exports, the leading export of Mali in 1965 was live animals, with smoked, dried, and salted fish coming in second, cotton third, and peanuts fourth. Other important intra-West African agricultural exports were meat, hides and skins, salt, and vegetables (see Table 30). The importance of the Office du Niger as a commercial supplier of rice and cotton and, in addition, as a future supplier of sugar cane should be noted. This state-run agency, which was created by the French in 1932 to develop the Inland Delta region of the middle Niger Valley, produces approximately 40 per cent of the commercialized cotton (7,700 out of 19,982 tons in 1963) and approximately two-thirds (20,000 tons) of the commercialized rice crop in Mali. The First Five Year Development Plan of Mali called for the planting of 4,000 hectares of sugar cane and for a greater emphasis

TABLE 30   Value of Recorded Exports of Mali for 1965
(*In Malian Francs*)

Commodity	Value	%
Live animals	1,277,703,000	33.0
Salted, dried, and smoked fish	771,915,000	19.9
Cotton	658,466,000	17.0
Oil seeds	625,500,000	16.1
Meats	61,482,000	1.6
Hides and skins	40,720,000	1.1
Salt and other minerals	34,978,000	0.9
Tobacco and tobacco products	22,764,000	0.6
Vegetables	19,135,000	0.5
Other	364,522,000	9.4
Total	3,877,185,000	100.0

Note: 245 Malian francs equal one U.S. dollar.
Source: République du Mali, Ministère d'État Chargé du Plan et de la Coordination des Affaires Économiques et Financières, Service de la Statistique Générale et de la Comptabilité Économique Nationale, *Bulletin Mensuel de Statistique*, No. 1 (Janvier-Février 1966), p. 39.

to be placed upon the production of cotton within the program of the agency. However, unlike the original Office du Niger development plans, which called for this scheme to supply virtually all the cotton needs of France, the current surplus production of rice, cotton, sugar cane, and other crops is (and will be) used almost entirely to satisfy local Malian needs or for export to other West African states, notably Senegal. With the reopening of the former Dakar-Niger Railroad, the traditional movement of Malian cotton to the textile plants of the Cape Verde industrial complex and rice to help satisfy the food deficit problem of Senegal has been resumed. It is very unlikely that, under present development plans, the Office du Niger will contribute significantly to the future cargo loading pattern at the port of Dakar; once again, the element of distance is the controlling factor.[54]

And finally, the problem of distance from the coast is also a handicap to any large-scale mineral-development projects in Mali. Geological prospection is still in its early stages, and so far no significant discoveries have been made. Low-grade phosphate deposits, however, have been discovered near Gao; and mineral deposits of iron, lead, aluminum, zinc, copper, tin, tungsten, manganese, molybdenum, and gold have been found, although not in sufficient quantities to lead to serious consideration of exploitation. In addition the sedimentary rock that overlies much of the ancient crystalline base of the country does have petroleum potential. At present the only mineral deposits being worked are the famous salt deposits at Taoudéni in the northern Saharan region of the country, with no other development plans yet under way.

Thus, while independence has witnessed a weakening of the colonially induced dependence of Mali upon its traditional overseas outlet of the port of Dakar, the immediate apparent effect (except for the 34-month period when all commercial movements between Senegal and Mali were cut off) has been slight. Since independence, a new Malian free-trade zone has been established in the South Zone of the port of Dakar, and virtually no more Malian trade passes through the port of Kaolack. The volume of Malian trade passing through the port of Dakar is approximately at the pre-independence level. Although the absolute volume of cargo movements has not changed much, the relative importance of Senegal in the overseas-trade-movement pattern of Mali has decreased. The improvement of old roads and the development of new road ties with Upper Volta and the Ivory Coast during the period of the Mali-Senegal estrangement has led to the apparently permanent diversion of much of the overseas trade of Mali to the port of Abidjan, with approximately one-quarter to one-third of Mali's overseas movements passing through Abidjan today. The corresponding percentage prior to 1960 was approximately 10 per cent.

The Mauritanian Hinterland

Although about 50 per cent of what is now the Dakar hinterland lies within Mauritania, this largely desert and sahelian country accounts for approximately 10 per cent of the cargo movements passing through the port. In addition, as the Mauritanian maritime outlets of Port Étienne and Nouakchott become better developed in terms of facilities and hinterland transportation connections, the dependence of Mauritania upon the port of Dakar will be greatly reduced. In the future it is very likely that virtually all the exports of Mauritania will pass through Port Étienne and over the wharf at Nouakchott, and that only a limited amount of imports (notably petroleum products, flour, and heavy equipment) will continue to pass through the port of Dakar. The first step in this direction was taken in February 1963, when it was decreed that all goods moving on Mauritanian roads must move on Mauritanian-registered carriers, with exceptions being made for bulk petroleum carriers and others where the transshipment of the freight at the border would be difficult. The immediate effect of this ruling was felt hardest by Senegalese truckers moving commodities to Mauritania directly from Dakar or from the railheads at Saint Louis and Linguère. With the development of a better internal road network, it is very likely that Mauritanian nationalism will lead to a similar decree calling for virtually all overseas trade to pass via the country's two maritime outlets.

Since Senegal and Mauritania have a complete customs union, it is difficult to determine exactly the value and volume of Mauritania's overseas trade; it is even more difficult to determine the extent of this trade passing through the port of Dakar. There are no customs formalities upon crossing the Senegal River and entering one country from the other; Mauritania and Senegal divide customs receipts at the port of Dakar at a pre-agreed ratio, with Mauritania today getting 8.66 per cent. (Official Mauritanian foreign-trade and customs statistics include

FIG. 34 The ferry connecting Senegal (across the Senegal River) and Mauritania (foreground)

only those commodities passing directly through Mauritanian customs, notably at Port Étienne and Nouakchott.) Taking this figure and applying it to the total volume of imports entering through the port of Dakar in 1965, one can say with some degree of accuracy that Mauritanian imports passing through the port amounted to approximately 80,000 tons in 1965. It is difficult to verify this figure by examining Senegalese transportation statistics, since many of these imports are carried by private trucks to Mauritania either directly from Dakar or after first moving by rail to Saint Louis, Linguère, or, since the opening of the rail line between Senegal and Mali, Kayes. The only statistics available are those of the Senegal Railroad and the Société Anonyme des Messageries du Sénégal (MESSAGAL), which provides scheduled passenger and cargo service on the Senegal River between Saint Louis and Bakel. An examination of these statistics shows that during the 1964–1965 fiscal year, 45,000 tons of merchandise were transported by rail to Saint Louis and 5,000 tons by rail to Linguère, much of which, however, was for Senegalese consumption, while in 1965, MESSAGAL unloaded 15,058 tons of cargo at Mauritanian river ports.[55] Much of the freight moving from Dakar to Mauritania, however, consists of products of local Cape Verde industries (cement, shoes, flour, etc.) and not imports (at least as such) passing through the port. Thus by accepting the 8.66 per cent figure, we have a fairly good approximation of the value (and thus with less accuracy, the volume) of Mauritanian imports passing through the port of Dakar.

It is difficult to calculate exactly the total volume of Mauritanian exports as well as those passing through the port of Dakar. The reason for this is, once again, the free movement of goods between Senegal and Mauritania. Detailed statistics are available only for exports (and imports) passing through customs at Port Étienne and Nouakchott. On the basis of available information, annual exports are approximately as follows:

1. Iron ore: 5,963,000 tons in 1965 (expected to reach 7,500,000 tons by 1968) from the Société Anonyme des Mines de Fer de Mauritanie (MIFERMA) operations at Fort Gouraud, all passing through Port Étienne;

2. Fish (salted and dried): approximately 3,000 tons annually, all passing through Port Étienne;

3. Livestock: close to one million head (chiefly sheep and goats), passing on foot to neighboring countries;

4. Gum arabic: approximately 3,000 tons from the southern sahelian region, most of which is exported through the port of Dakar; and

5. Less than 1,000 tons of miscellaneous commodities, such as peanuts from "the Chemame"—that is, the valley of the Senegal River. Thus one can safely say that Mauritania accounts for less than 5,000 tons of cargo embarkations annually at the port of Dakar. There is little likelihood that this trade via Dakar will increase in the future; with the improvement of the Mauritanian road web, it will very likely decrease as the wharf at Nouakchott exerts its pull.

Under the terms of the new Four Year Development Plan (1963–1966), among other things, the wharf at Nouakchott was to be built (already completed) and the road network was to be expanded, including bituminizing the Trans-Mauritania Highway from Nouakchott to Rosso and extending the existing limited network in the southern, agriculturally more productive part of the country. When this new transportation web is completed, it is virtually certain that most of the overseas trade of Mauritania that is today passing through Dakar will be diverted to Port Étienne and Nouakchott and that all future development schemes, such as the exploitation of the copper deposits at Akjoujt will be pursued within this framework. Thus within a few years the port of Dakar will very probably, with the exception of a few specialized imports, lose the Mauritanian hinterland to Port Étienne and Nouakchott. In terms of the existing cargo-loading and -unloading pattern, this will mean a loss of approximately 85,000 tons annually, although in terms of future handlings the figure would be considerably higher.

Therefore, while the areal extent of the Dakar hinterland is today substantially the same as it was prior to 1960, new forces are in the process of modifying the details of the port–hinterland relationship. In the foreseeable future the details will very probably add up to a substantial modification in this induced relationship. It is very likely that the future will witness also the virtual severance of Mauritania from the

Dakar hinterland, a continued weakening (though not a complete separation) of the induced ties between Mali and the port of Dakar, and a modification in the present-day intra-Senegalese movement of commodities from or destined to overseas ports. The big uncertainty in this regard is the future role to be played by the port of Bathurst. A political and economic federation between Senegal and the Gambia would open up this port to Senegalese (and Malian)traffic. While it is virtually certain that such an eventuality would sound the knell for the ports of Ziguinchor and Kaolack, its effect upon the port of Dakar is much more problematical. It is very unlikely that Bathurst would be allowed to (or could) develop as a serious competitor to the well-entrenched and powerful port of Dakar. Its chief role would be to drain most of the peanuts of Sine-Saloum, the Rip, and Casamance now passing through Kaolack and Ziguinchor, and possibly become a supplemental drainer of Mali. In any event, the hinterland of the port of Dakar is in the process of modifying the colonially induced pattern, a change that could come about only by the modification of the transportation links that have in the past bound Dakar firmly to approximately one-third of West Africa.

6 / Conclusion

THE PORT of Dakar is in the process of assuming a new role in independent West Africa. Perhaps more accurately, a new set of forces has been introduced in West Africa which is forcing the port of Dakar to modify its traditional role in the region. Prior to 1960 Dakar was the leading port of West Africa (as well as of the territories of former French West Africa) in terms of total tonnage handled. It was also an important exporter of manufactured goods to the other states of Africa (notably those of French-speaking West and Equatorial Africa) and one of the world's leading bunkering centers. In terms of areal extent, it served the largest hinterland of any of the ports of West Africa, serving approximately one-third of the total region. It achieved this distinction through a combination of fortuitous factors, both physical and cultural. In physical terms, the port of Dakar lies on the extreme western protrusion of continental Africa close to important Atlantic trade routes: those going from North America to the west, southern, and east coasts of Africa, and those going from Europe to southern South America and western and southern Africa. This location factor, coupled with excellent site factors, led to Dakar's development as one of the world's foremost bunkering centers. Although competition for this trade in the past has come chiefly from the Canary Islands, and more serious competition will probably come in the future from Freetown and perhaps some other ports of West Africa, it is very unlikely that this function of the port of Dakar will be modified substantially in the future. Independence has had (and very probably will have) little or no effect upon this role of the port. The factors of location and site, the excellent bunkering facilities

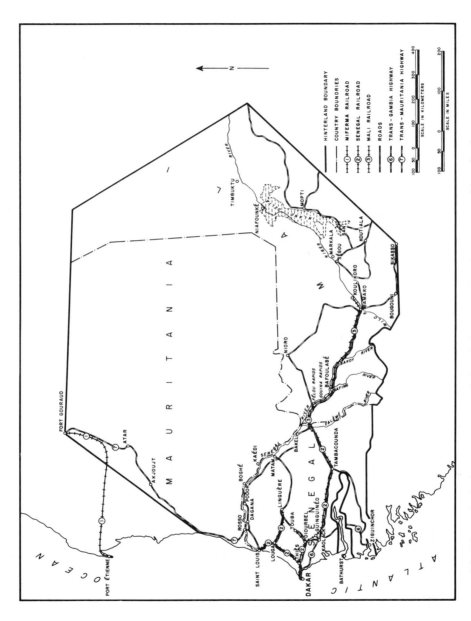

FIG. 35 The principal transportation links of the Port of Dakar with its hinterland

Régie des Chemins de Fer du Sénégal (the Senegal Railroad) and its continuation in the Republic of Mali, the Régie des Chemins de Fer du Mali (the Mali Railroad). This main trunk line also connects Dakar with the upper course of the Senegal River at Kayes in Mali, while the Dakar-Saint Louis rail line links the port with the lower course of the river at Saint Louis. As a result of this railroad network, the coordinated use of the two rivers, and the construction of direct and feeder road connections, the port of Dakar has evolved as the primary maritime outlet for a vast hinterland of approximately 1,800,000 square kilometers (700,000 square miles).

The Railroad

The Senegal River and the port of Saint Louis formed the original route contemplated for the exploitation of the vast Sudanese interior under French control. The difficulties of breaching the shifting sandbar at the mouth of the Senegal River in order to reach the port, the seasonal limitations of navigation on the river, and the generally unproductive immediate hinterland in terms of the requirements of European industry combined to preclude the development of Saint Louis as the major port of the French holdings in West Africa. Consequently, emphasis was shifted further south to the vicinity of Cape Verde Peninsula. In 1882 work was begun by the joint public-private Compagnie de Chemin de Fer de Dakar à Saint-Louis on the construction of a railroad between Saint Louis and Dakar, to pass through the then restive but potentially very productive region of the Cayor. With the encouragement of the French government in the form of favorable leases and financial guaranties, this 264-kilometer line was completed in 1885. Though a limited success at first, this standard meter-gauge railroad (as are all the railroads in former French West Africa) enjoyed a financial boom following the complete pacification of the Cayor and its development during the early years of this century into the then major peanut-producing region of Senegal. To capitalize on this by expanding the productive peanut-producing area, the 129-kilometer Linguère-Louga spur was completed just prior to World War I. The Cayor region, however, soon suffered the fate common to most overdeveloped peanut regions—the depletion of its soils. With the decrease in soil fertility and the construction of new rail lines further south, the principal peanut-producing regions of Senegal moved to the newly opened areas.

Concomitant with the development of the Cayor was the development of the port of Dakar and the decline of the port of Saint Louis. Today Saint Louis is utilized almost solely as the transshipment river port for merchandise moving between Dakar and the economically dormant Senegal River Valley and Mauritania, using the Dakar-Saint Louis rail line and the new paved highway as the connecting links. Thus the Dakar-Saint Louis rail line and the spur to Linguère have two principal commercial functions: (1) to help service the Senegal River Valley and Mauritania via the port of Dakar; and (2) to drain, also to Dakar, the remaining peanut production of the Cayor. During the 1964–1965 fiscal year,[2] 45,000 tons of general cargo and 222,000 passengers detrained at St. Louis, while 3,000 tons of cargo (chiefly millet, gum arabic, peanuts, and empty containers) and 222,000 passengers entrained at the city.[3]

Since independence, two factors have emerged to further reduce the importance of this rail line in the economic picture of the region: (1) Mauritanian nationalism, which has led to the construction of the new wharf at Nouakchott and the port at Port Etienne and the eventual divergence of most of Mauritania's overseas trade from Dakar to them; and (2) the new paved highway linking Dakar, Saint Louis, and Rosso, which has diverted much of the passenger and freight traffic to "car-rapids" and trucks. In terms of long-range planning, however, the carrying out of the development schemes for the Senegal River Valley could lead to a revitalization of Saint Louis and this railroad, although the development of a new maritime port at Saint Louis could lead to a still further economic decline of this line.

In 1881 work was begun on the 555-kilometer Kayes-Niger River link of what is now the Régie des Chemins de Fer du Mali. It was hoped that this connection from the Niger River at Koulikoro in French Sudan (present-day Mail) to the Senegal River at Kayes, also in French Sudan, would stimulate the production and evacuation of commercial crops from the potentially productive Niger River Valley via the Senegal River and the port of Saint Louis. This government-sponsored project encountered numerous financial and personnel difficulties (for example, a yellow fever epidemic in 1900 and 1901 caused widespread havoc among the workers) before being completed in 1904. However, difficulties of navigation on the Niger River, similar difficulties on the Senegal River, and the factor of distance combined to limit the immediate contribution of this railroad to Senegalese port movements. It did, nevertheless, facilitate the evacuation of some commercial crops (notably peanuts, rice, and gum arabic) from French Sudan to Senegal, and ease the importation of goods to this landlocked territory. Also from a military and strategic point of view it was considered a great success.

Even before the completion of the Kayes-Koulikoro rail line, the colonial authorities recognized the deficiencies in terms of time and costs that a double transshipment of goods moving from the Niger Valley to Dakar or Rufisque (and vice versa) via the new railroad, the Senegal River, and the Dakar-Saint Louis Railroad would entail. In addition, the seasonality of navigation on the Senegal River added an additional burden to such a movement of goods. Consequently, a study was undertaken in 1902 to determine the feasibility of connecting Kayes directly with Thiès, a point on the Dakar-Saint Louis Railroad, and thus link Dakar directly by rail with the Niger River Valley. A favorable report being submitted, work on this 663-kilometer stretch was begun in 1909. Because of delays occasioned by World War I, it was not completed until 1923. Two additional spurs from the main line, the 21-kilometer Guinguinéo-Kaolack spur completed in 1912 and the 47-kilometer Diourbel-Touba spur opened in 1931, completed the basic railroad pattern of Senegal and French Sudan. The immediate effect of this new main line and the two spurs was to stimulate commercial peanut production in the Baol (the region of Senegal south of the Cayor and north of the Saloum Estuary), and to increase it to a lesser extent in the Rip (the region of Senegal between the Saloum Estuary and the Gambia), the Boundou (the region of eastern Senegal), and French Sudan. The principal commercial role of the Dakar-Koulikoro rail line is still basically the same today: to drain the commercial peanut production (plus a limited amount of other commodities) of these regions to the ports of Dakar and Kaolack and to service eastern Senegal and Mali.

In 1933 these various rail lines were united under a single public administration, the Région Dakar-Niger, one of the four divisions of the

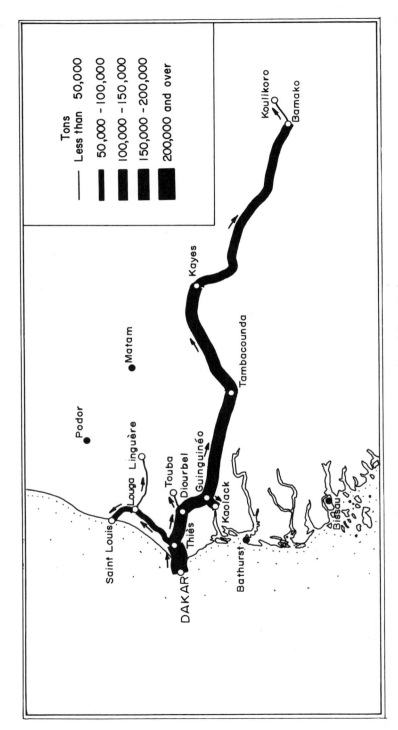

FIG. 36 Merchandise movement on the Dakar–Niger Railroad from Dakar
to the interior for 1959

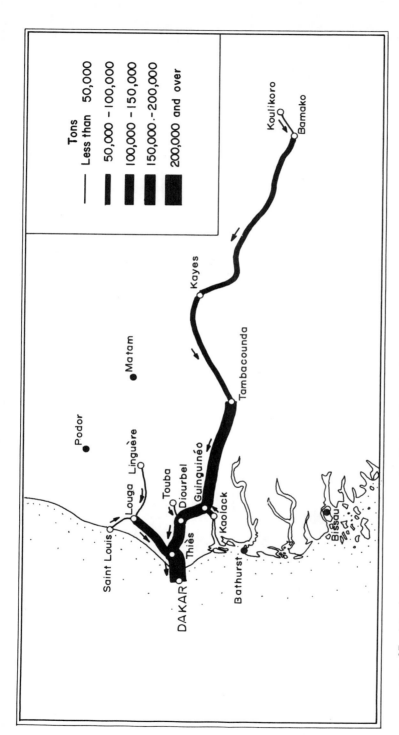

FIG. 37   Merchandise movement on the Dakar–Niger Railroad from the
interior to Dakar for 1959

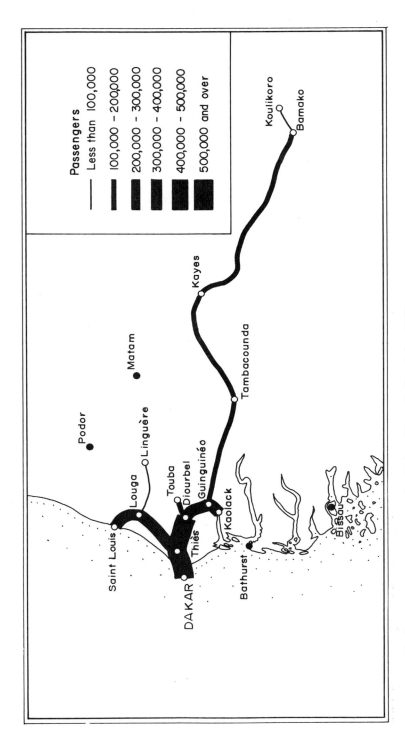

FIG. 38   Passenger movements on the Dakar–Niger Railroad for 1959

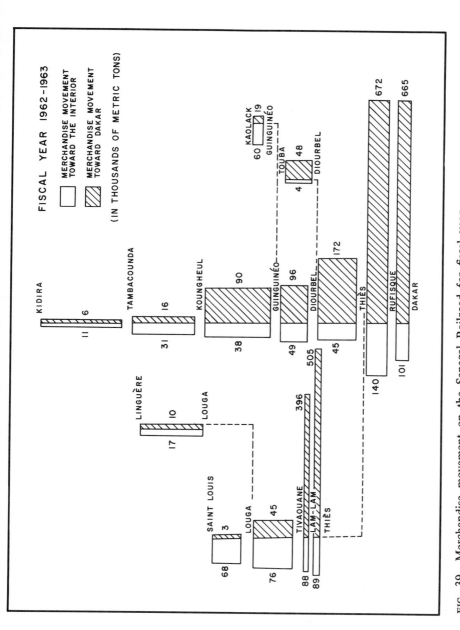

FIG. 39 Merchandise movement on the Senegal Railroad for fiscal year 1962–1963

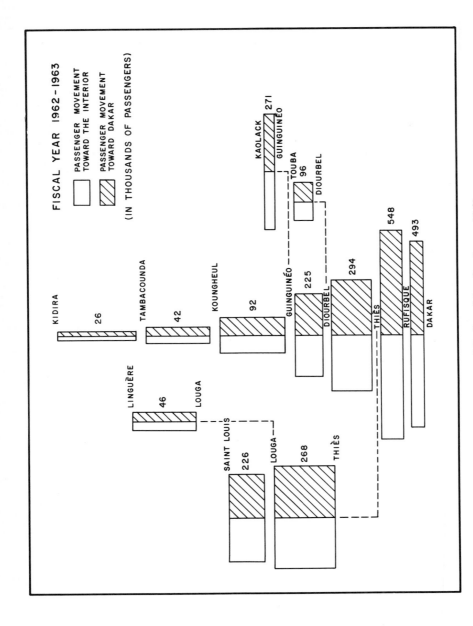

FISCAL YEAR 1962–1963

PASSENGER MOVEMENT
TOWARD THE INTERIOR

PASSENGER MOVEMENT
TOWARD DAKAR

(IN THOUSANDS OF PASSENGERS)

KIDIRA 26

TAMBACOUNDA 42

KOUNGHEUL 92

GUINGUINÉO 225

DIOURBEL 294

THIÈS 548

RUFISQUE 493

DAKAR

KAOLACK 271

GUINGUINÉO

TOUBA 96

DIOURBEL

GUINGUINÉO

LINGUÈRE 46

LOUGA

SAINT LOUIS 226

LOUGA

THIÈS 268

THIÈS

FIG. 40   Passenger movements on the Senegal Railroad for fiscal year 1962–1963

Régie Fédérale des Chemins de Fer de l'Afrique Occidentale Française.[4] At its dissolution in 1960 (at the time of the rupture of the Mali Federation), this division had a total of 1,678 kilometers of track (excluding the 21 kilometers of track within the port of Dakar and double-counting the 56 kilometers of double track between Thiès and Dakar) under its jurisdiction. In 1959 [5] this unified system brought 255,000 tons of merchandise (mainly peanuts and phosphates) to Dakar and carried away 220,000 tons of miscellaneous goods to the interior. It also brought 123,000 tons of merchandise (almost entirely peanuts) to the port of Kaolack via the Guinguinéo-Kaolack spur, which also moved 64,000 tons of miscellaneous goods into eastern Senegal and former French Sudan (see Figs. 36, 37, and 38).

In 1960 the Dakar-Niger Railroad was split into two separate systems, the Régie des Chemins de Fer du Sénégal, with 1,033 kilometers of track, and the Régie des Chemins de Fer du Mali, with 645 kilome-

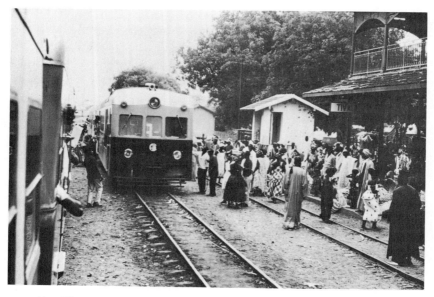

FIG. 41 The Dakar–Saint Louis branch of the Senegal Railroad at Tivaouane

ters of track. During the 1962–1963 fiscal year, only the former fed the port of Dakar, and showed the following statistics:[6]

Passengers carried	3,928,676
Passenger-kilometers traveled	294,952,039
Merchandise carried	948,363
Phosphates	451,868
Peanuts	248,466
Miscellaneous goods	248,029
Ton-kilometers traveled	138,326,975

It is very difficult to calculate exactly the loss to the Senegal rail system brought about by the cutting of the rail line between Senegal and Mali. In 1959 approximately 167,000 tons of miscellaneous goods entered the railroad station at Kayes in Mali from Senegal, while approximately 90,000 tons (an estimated 40 per cent being peanuts) crossed the fron-

FIG. 42   The Mali Railroad and the railroad station at Bamako, Mali

tier in the opposite direction.[7] Thus using these figures, and interpolating on the basis of a moderate growth in the economy of Mali during the subsequent three years, one can safely estimate the annual loss to be close to 300,000 tons. It should be noted, however, that much of this traffic did not originate from nor was destined to Dakar or Kaolack, but consisted of local movements of cattle, fish, small grains, and other commodities.

TABLE 31   Volume of Freight Moved by the Régie des Chemins de Fer du Sénégal (the Senegal Railroad) for 1961 and Fiscal Year 1964–1965
(In Metric Tons)

Commodities	*1961*		*1964–1965*	
	Tons	*%*	*Tons*	*%*
Phosphates	569,168	56.6	840,992	59.2
Peanuts	254,405	25.3	247,672	17.4
Peanut oil, peanut cake, and other peanut derivatives	9,530	0.9	1,999	0.1
Other oil seeds	145	. . .	. . .	. . .
Construction materials and other industrial goods	27,066	2.7	78,694	5.5
Petroleum products	29,784	3.0	69,256	4.9
Flour and other non-perishable foodstuffs	1,728	0.2	} 20,289	} 1.4
Perishable foodstuffs	2,404	0.2		
Fertilizer	6,685	0.7	1,386	0.1
Live animals	5,137	0.5	4,689	0.3
Salt	186	. . .	9,400	0.7
Empty containers	1,189	0.1	2,029	0.1
Solid fuels	4,467	0.4	415	. . .
Forage and straw	587	0.1	799	0.1
Mangoes	645	0.1	. . .	. . .
Other commodities	93,205	9.3	142,607	10.0
Total	1,006,331	100.0	1,420,227	100.0

Sources: (*a*) République du Sénégal, Ministère du Plan et du Développement, Service de la Statistique, *Bulletin Statistique et Économique Mensuel*, Année 1963-No. 12 (Décembre 1963) (Dakar: Grande Imprimerie Africaine, 1964), p. 16; and (*b*) République du Sénégal, Ministère des Travaux Publics, de l'Urbanisme et des Transports, Régie des Chemins de Fer du Sénégal, *Compte Rendu de Gestion 1964–65* (Thiès: Imprimerie Chemins de Fer, 1965), Tables 12 and 12 bis.

TABLE 32   Volume of Freight Moved by the Régie des Chemins de Fer du Mali (the Mali Railroad) for 1961 and 1965

(*In Metric Tons*)

Commodity	1961		1965	
	Tons	*%*	*Tons*	*%*
Cement	. . .	. . .	41,644	17.0
Petroleum products	. . .	. . .	30,230	12.4
Decorticated peanuts	24,256	40.9	20,138	8.2
Undecorticated peanuts	1,733	2.9	814	0.3
Peanut cake	452	0.8	4,002	1.6
Peanut oil	61	0.1	90	. . .
Millet	701	1.2	3,579	1.5
Cotton	8	. . .	3,419	1.4
Cola nuts	3,080	5.2	2,670	1.1
Local wood	. . .	. . .	2,073	0.8
Salt	1,343	2.3	1,428	0.6
Rice	8,327	14.0	1,357	0.6
Live animals	930	1.6	883	0.4
Shea butter	12	. . .	406	0.2
Hides and skins	57	0.1	398	0.2
Soap	. . .	. . .	241	0.1
Tobacco products	111	0.2	163	0.1
Gum arabic	208	0.4	143	0.1
Fertilizer	. . .	. . .	130	0.1
Wool	. . .	. . .	72	. . .
Straw mats	48	0.1	22	. . .
Shea kernels	36	0.1	. . .	. . .
Kapok	14	. . .	. . .	. . .
Construction material and miscellaneous	17,973	30.3	130,487	53.4
Total	59,350	100.0	244,389	100.0

Sources: (*a*) Chambre de Commerce, d'Agriculture et d'Industrie de Bamako (République du Mali), *Annuaire Statistique 1961 de la République du Mali*, Août 1962, p. 5; and (*b*) République du Mali, Ministère d'État Chargé du Plan et de la Coordination des Affaires Économiques et Financières, Service de la Statistique Générale et de la Comptabilité Économique Nationale, *Bulletin Mensuel de Statistique*, No. 1 (Janvier-Février 1966), p. 8.

The effect of the split upon rail movements in Mali was more striking. In 1959 freight movements on the stretch of the Dakar-Niger Railroad in present-day Mali amounted to 200,000 to 300,000 tons. In 1961 this had dropped to 59,350 tons (see Table 32). The pattern of trade had shifted from Senegal to Upper Volta, the Ivory Coast, and Guinea, with the consequent increase in dependence upon motor transportation.

With the reopening of the Senegal-Mali rail line in July 1963, a study[8] was made by the Senegal Railroad to determine the effect that this would have upon merchandise movements between Dakar and Mali. It showed that in 1964, despite the development of new ties over the preceding three years, the port of Dakar was once again the leading maritime outlet for Mali, but that an estimated 40,000 tons of cargo annually that formerly would have moved through the port of Dakar now passed through the port of Abidjan in the Ivory Coast. This movement of goods is conditioned by three factors: (1) economics (the southern region of Mali can be serviced more economically through Abidjan); (2) a conscious effort to maintain these new outlets and thus eliminate the former virtual sole dependence upon the port of Dakar; and (3) balance of payments difficulties with Senegal. In regard to this last factor, the complementary nature of the economies of Mali and the Ivory Coast should be noted, thus enabling Mali to export more to the latter than to Senegal, whose economy is basically the same as Mali's. It was further estimated that during the 1964–1965 fiscal year, Mali would be moving approximately 56,000 tons of freight by rail to Dakar, and that 144,000 tons (an estimated 12,000 tons per month) would move from Dakar to the landlocked republic. Actual traffic during that year came fairly close to the amount predicted (compare Tables 33 and 34).

Most of the overseas trade of Mali passing through Senegal now passes through Mali's free port located in the South Zone of the port of Dakar (see Chapter 3), with a consequent loss to the port of Kaolack. Before the Senegal-Mali estrangement, French Sudan (Mali) accounted for approximately 10 to 20 per cent of the cargo embarkations at Kaolack. Thus, since the reopening of the rail line between Senegal and Mali, the port of Dakar has recaptured most of the Malian hinterland, but has lost an estimated 40,000 tons of cargo to the port of Abidjan. At the same time it has acquired virtually all of Mali's overseas trade

TABLE 33   Estimated Railroad Freight Movements between Dakar and Mali for
Fiscal Year 1964–1965

(In Metric Tons)

Movements from Dakar to Mali		*Movements from Mali to Dakar*	
Petroleum products	30,000	Peanuts	40,000
Cement	30,000	Rice and millet	10,000
Construction material	20,000	Cotton	3,000
Miscellaneous groceries	10,000	Miscellaneous	3,000
Salt	15,000		
Drinks	5,000		
Miscellaneous	34,000		
Total	144,000	Total	56,000

Source: République du Sénégal, Ministère des Travaux Publics, de l'Urbanisme, de
l'Habitat, et des Transports, Régie des Chemins de Fer du Sénégal, *Budget d'Exploitation—Exercice 1964–1965* (Thiès: Imprimerie Chemins de Fer, 1964), p. 4.

that formerly passed through the port of Kaolack (an estimated 20,000
to 40,000 tons).

The Dakar-Niger Railroad, with a view to providing an integrated
service between the port of Dakar and various inland destinations, coordinated its services with those of the Société des Messageries du Séné-

TABLE 34   Freight Carried by the Senegal Railroad between Senegal and Mali
for Fiscal Year 1964–1965

(In Metric Tons)

Movements from Senegal to Mali		*Movements from Mali to Senegal*	
Cement	45,766	Peanuts	25,954
Petroleum products	37,610	Millet	3,325
Construction material	17,898	Cotton and kapok	2,913
Miscellaneous groceries	15,398	Empty containers	2,029
Salt	9,400	Peanut cake	1,999
Fertilizer	1,386	Shea butter	1,809
Drinks	1,004	Hides and skins	536
Miscellaneous	11,750	Miscellaneous	1,021
Total	140,212	Total	39,586

Source: République du Sénégal, Ministère des Travaux Publics, de l'Urbanisme et des
Transports, Régie des Chemins de Fer du Sénégal, *Compte Rendu de Gestion 1964–65*
(Thiès: Imprimerie Chemins de Fer, 1965), Table 12 bis.

gal, which runs scheduled river-boat service on the Senegal River between Saint Louis and Bakel (and sometimes Kayes), the former Société des Messageries Africaines,[9] which provided a similar service on the Niger River between Koulikoro and Gao, and the Compagnie Transafricaine, the largest trucking concern operating in the central Sudan. This coordination of services has largely been continued under the new divisions of the railroad. In 1960 it was generally agreed that the facilities of and the services provided by the Dakar-Niger Railroad were far superior (though more costly) than those of the Abidjan-Niger Railroad, the other major competitor for the trade of middle Niger Valley.[10] The reason for this was the fact that severe road competition in the Ivory Coast and Upper Volta (where the principal north-south road from Abidjan to Ouagadougou via Bouaké and Bobo-Dioulasso runs virtually parallel with the railroad) forced the railroad tariffs to be lowered greatly. The result was a chronic deficit, the use of outmoded equipment, numerous breakdowns, and generally poor service. The Dakar-Niger Railroad, on the other hand, was able to compensate for the higher tariffs by providing better service and by the fact that its two maritime outlets, the ports of Dakar and Kaolack, were located much closer to Europe than the port of Abidjan.

With the recent expansion and improvement of the road network in Senegal (including roads running virtually parallel with the railroad), the Senegal Railroad has also begun to experience severe truck competition. By 1963 it was estimated that, exclusive of phosphate movements (which move entirely by rail to storage facilities in the Northwest Zone of the port of Dakar), trucks accounted for more than twice the volume of freight movements than the railroad.[11] To meet this challenge, tariffs on this line also have been reduced (although still considerably higher in 1965 than on the Abidjan-Niger Railroad), with the result that there was an operating deficit of 620 million francs CFA (2,530,000 U.S. dollars) during the 1964–1965 fiscal year.[12] To erase this deficit, it has been suggested that the unprofitable Louga-Linguère spur be closed, and plans have been advanced to stop all future investments in passenger service and to progressively transfer passenger traffic from rail to road transportation while encouraging the movement of goods by rail by increasing road taxes and by giving the railroad exclusive rights to move goods between certain points.[13] Owing to the fact that it is virtually impossible to travel by road between Kayes and Bamako, this problem has not yet been faced by the Mali Railroad.

Future development plans for the two rail systems have been clouded by the recent political estrangement between Mali and Senegal. There are no definite plans, however, for the extension of existing facilities in either country, although the nature of the topography in both countries (as well as in Mauritania) is such that no serious physiographic difficulties to the expansion of the rail network exist. The controlling factor (other than the availability of capital) in each case is one of economic justification, the nature of the hinterland and/or its distance from the coast largely limiting the expansion and intensification of land use in an area. Although the Senegal Railroad is not contemplating the extension of its lines, it is planning, under the provisions of the First and Second Four Year Plans, to improve existing facilities. More stretches (particularly along the most heavily traveled section between Thiès and Dakar) are to be double tracked, new stations are to be built, new equipment is to be bought, and the safety factor is to be improved. The plans for the Mali Railroad are more problematical. In addition to improving existing facilities, plans are still being considered (although at the moment remote) for the construction of a rail line connecting Bamako with Kouroussa in Guinea via the valley of the upper Niger River, and thus linking the Mali Railroad with the Chemin de Fer de Guinée (Guinea Railroad) and the port of Conakry.[14] Preliminary surveys for this projected railroad have been completed by Soviet engineers, with a favorable report submitted. Such an additional rail outlet would further reduce the dependence of landlocked Mali upon a single rail outlet, and would divert some of the overseas trade of Mali from Dakar (and probably Abidjan) to Conakry. However, the reopening of the railroad to Dakar has removed the urgency of this project, while the poor state of repairs of the Guinea Railroad has made it less attractive, and so definite construction plans have not yet been announced. And finally, it should be noted that the plans advanced by the former colonial authorities to connect eventually the Dakar-Niger and the Abidjan-Niger railroads by means of a line extending from Bamako to Bobo-Dioulasso and to extend the Dakar-Niger line from Koulikoro to Ségou and beyond have now virtually been abandoned by the new independent governments. Such a coordinated plan of development, it was felt, would have opened the entire middle Niger Valley to a more intensive level of commercial economic development.

The Road Network

In addition to the railroad, the port of Dakar is fed to a large, though undetermined, extent by motor transportation. However, road construction in former French West Africa was planned and developed subordinate to the railroad, which was to be the most important feeder of the port. Consequently the prewar road system evolved largely as a feeder system to the Niger River and the Dakar-Niger Railroad. The result was a system of poorly planned and constructed roads that often became flooded and/or suffered severe damage during the rainy season and which over the course of time developed the "phénomène de la tôle ondulée," a term used throughout former French Africa to describe the condition of lateritic roads which have developed closely spaced parallel ridges running perpendicular to the main axis of the road. Postwar road-development programs have, however, moved away from this original concept, and a well-constructed though still limited road network is evolving in its own right, often providing direct competition to the railroad. Largely through funds made available in recent years by France through the Fonds d'Investissement et de Développement Économique et Social des Territoires d'Outremer (FIDES) and its successor, the Fonds d'Aide et de Cooperation (FAC), and by aid provided in more recent years by the Development Fund of the European Economic Community, the basic road and trail networks of Senegal, Mali, and Mauritania consist of approximately the following:

	Senegal	Mali	Mauritania
Total road and trail networks (km)	14,338	12,000	5,870
Bituminized roads (km)	1,861	665	0
Dirt roads (km)	1,477	. . .	2,170
Dirt trails (km)	11,000	. . .	3,700

The densest road network is found in the regions of greatest economic interest—the western one-third of Senegal from where most of the peanut and phosphate embarkations at the port of Dakar originate and in southern Mali. It should be noted that dirt-road construction is facilitated by the presence of lateritic soils south of a line drawn roughly from Dakar to Niamey in Niger and passing through Bamako, Ségou, and Mopti, and made more difficult by the presence of largely unconsolidated sand to the north.

In Senegal the principal roads, as one would expect, radiate from Dakar (see Fig. 35). These main arteries are: (1) Federal Route 1 (the Route du Soudan), which goes from Dakar to the Mali frontier via Kaolack and Tambacounda, and which is bituminized to 65 kilometers beyond Kaolack; (2) Federal Route 3, which extends from Dakar to Saint Louis to Rosso and continues in Mauritania as the Trans-Mauritania Highway, and which is bituminized to Rosso; and (3) the Trans-Gambia Highway, an embranchment at Kaolack of Federal Route 1, which is bituminized to Ziguinchor and which has succeeded in capturing most of the Casamance trade for Dakar. The first two roads parallel the two main lines of the Senegal Railroad and have in recent years taken away much of its trade. Today most of the commercial peanut crop of Senegal (whose production is concentrated in western Senegal, notably in the Baol, Sine-Saloum, the Rip, and Casamance) moves by road to the peanut-oil plants or the ports, with railroad movements becoming more important the further east one goes.

Note should also be made of the recently completed dirt road from Linguère to Matam which, in conjunction with the otherwise little-used Louga-Linguère spur of the Senegal Railroad, helps tie southern Mauritania and the Senegal River Valley to Dakar; the seasonal Route de Casamance running the entire length of the province from Ziguinchor to Tambacounda and which was the principal overland route to Dakar before the completion of the Trans-Gambia Highway; and the seasonal Route du Fleuve which runs the length of the Senegal River in Senegal. In general, the basic road network of Senegal has been defined largely in terms of a colonial-export economy and has developed on that basis. It is generally adequate in servicing the needs of such an economy, but less than adequate in terms of year-round intra-Senegalese communication. Taking this into account, the First and Second Four Year Plans call for the improvement and extension of the remoter roads and trails such as those in the valley of the Senegal River and in the eastern part of the country.

The road network of Mali is less dense than that of Senegal, with the densest concentration in the southern part of the country, the region of greatest economic and demographic significance (see Fig. 35). In the northern sahelian and desert regions, a poor system of trails exists. Under French colonial rule, the Niger River and the Dakar-Niger Railroad were the principal evacuation routes of the territory, with roads playing a secondary, feeder role. The principal roads in the territory either converged at Bamako (the present-day bituminized roads to Bougouni and Ségou plus their extensions and the dirt roads to Nioro and Nara) or were found in the valley of the Niger River. Consequently, an interterritorial road network was poorly developed. However, during the period when the railroad to Dakar was closed, road transportation assumed a much more important role in the overseas trade movements of Mali, with the overseas imports and exports of the country moving mainly by truck between the commercial centers of Mali and the Abidjan-Niger Railroad and, to a much lesser extent, the Guinea Railroad. Even with the reopening of the Dakar rail link, the new pattern that developed between 1960 and 1963 will not be erased completely, since continued emphasis is being placed on the development of the road network in the southern regions of Bougouni, Sikasso, Koutiala, and San, and on linking the Niger River Valley with bituminized roads to the Abidjan-Niger Railroad at Bobo-Dioulasso in Upper Volta and Ouangolodougou in the Ivory Coast. Today, approximately 40,000 tons of overseas trade have been lost to the port of Dakar and are moving over these new roads to and from the port of Abidjan. And finally, note should be made of the fact that the former virtual monopoly of the privately owned Compagnie Transafricaine in the heavy trucking operations in Mali (complementing the small African operators) has been broken by the creation of the state-owned Régie des Transports Maliens.

Not much need (nor can) be said about the existing road system of Mauritania. Since this territory was never an important source of raw materials for the French economy and, in addition, is sparsely populated, little capital was expended in the development of a good system of internal transportation. The principal road is the Trans-Mauritania Highway, a generally poor dirt or sandy road leading from Rosso on the Senegal River to Algeria and Morocco via Nouakchott, Akjoujt, Atar, and Fort Gouraud, a distance of over 3,000 kilometers. With the aid of a 6.7 million dollar loan from the World Bank, the 200-kilometer stretch of this road from Rosso to Nouakchott will be hard-surfaced (total cost 10 million dollars) and will connect the new wharf at Nouakchott with the Senegal River Valley, the most populous and agriculturally productive region of Mauritania. When completed in 1969 it will be the first hard-surfaced road in Mauritania and will tend to drain the overseas trade from and to the Senegal River region of the country from Dakar to Nouakchott. This trade is today very limited (a small volume of peanuts and gum arabic) and its loss will have little effect upon cargo embarkations at Dakar.

Other roads and trails in Mauritania are generally concentrated in the southern part of the country, particularly in and extending from the Senegal River Valley. Like the Trans-Mauritania Highway, these roads are impassable for limited periods during the short summer rainy season. Unlike in Senegal, where a fairly good road system allows small private owners with a limited amount of capital to operate small trucks, the nature of the roads in Mauritania calls for the use of large, heavy-duty vehicles, the ownership of which is beyond the means of most small entrepreneurs. Consequently, most of the road movements in the country are in the hands of three companies: the long-established Établissements Lacombe, Établissements G. Nassour, and the Nouvelle Société National de Transport Mauritanien. It is hoped, however, that with the increase in national revenue now starting to be derived from the MIFERMA iron-ore operations at Fort Gouraud and, eventually, from the exploitation of the copper deposits at Akjoujt, an expanded and improved road web will develop. With the development and expansion of the road system in Mauritania plus the construction of the new port at Port Étienne and the new wharf at Nouakchott, the tendency will be to rely less on the traditional service routes of the Senegal River and the Senegal Railroad to the port of Dakar and more on the two national outlets. It is very probable that this combination will, in the very near future, divert most of the overseas trade of Mauritania from the port of Dakar.

Thus there has been a marked change in the nature and role of road transportation in the Dakar hinterland since independence. Instead of being almost entirely a feeder system to the main transportation trunk artery, the Niger River and the Dakar-Niger Railroad, the road system has evolved in its own right. In Senegal road transportation has, with the exception of phosphate movements, become the principal mover of merchandise and the principal feeder of the port of Dakar. An intensive and well-constructed road web has evolved in the productive western one-third of the country, with protrusions extending to the rest of the country. In Mali the largely rudimentary feeder-road system inherited by the independent government has been expanded and improved to become a fairly good international system connecting Mali with Upper Volta and the Ivory Coast (and the Abidjan-Niger Railroad), and has diverted to Abidjan much of the overseas trade of that landlocked republic from its traditional outlet of Dakar. In Mauritania the development of a road network coupled with the construction of new maritime outlets is in the process of reducing that country's traditional ties with Senegal and Dakar. Therefore the development and improvement of road networks in the three countries of the Dakar hinterland has been instrumental in modifying the colonially induced pattern of trade; no longer does virtually all the overseas trade of this vast hinterland drain to the Niger and Senegal rivers and the former Dakar-Niger Railroad. The expanded road web, especially in Mali and Mauritania, has had and/or will have a centrifugal effect in diverting some of this trade to the other outlets of Abidjan, possibly Conakry, Port Étienne, and Nouakchott.

River Transportation

The port of Dakar is also fed indirectly by the two great rivers of West Africa, the Senegal and the Niger. As was noted earlier, the overall development plan of the colonial authorities in former French West Africa was to coordinate railroad construction so as to take advantage of these natural water arteries. Owing largely to the difficulties of navigation on these rivers, the grandiose plans for such a fully integrated rail-river transportation system never materialized. Nevertheless, the rivers still serve to a limited extent as feeders to the railroads (and to a much lesser extent the roads) which in turn feed the port of Dakar.

Dakar is today the sole outlet for the entire valley of the Senegal River with the exception of a small percentage of peanut exports from the region of Bakel (which move through the port of Kaolack) and the now politically estranged, though unproductive, headwater regions in the Fouta Djalon massif of Guinea. The valley is served by Dakar either directly by rail and/or road or by the Senegal River through the diminishing intermediary role of the port of Saint Louis. With the decline of Saint Louis as a direct ocean outlet and the increase in the zone of attraction of Dakar, transportation links running perpendicular to the river valley and oriented to Dakar have developed in lieu of the natural river route leading to Saint Louis. These newer routes, as was noted earlier, are the Dakar-Saint Louis Railroad, Federal Route 3, the railroad spur from Louga to Linguère joined by the new road from Linguère to Matam, and the Dakar-Kayes link of the former Dakar-Niger Railroad. The Senegal River is still used to a limited extent, however, to move goods to and from Dakar.

The Senegal River has its source 1,400 kilometers from its mouth in the Fouta Djalon massif in the form of two eventually uniting tributaries, the Bafing and Bakoy rivers. The Senegal River proper is born at Bafoulabé in western Mali by the joining of these two branches. The river then passes over the rapids of Gouina and Félou (which determine the maximum navigable reaches of the river), flows through Kayes, and is joined approximately 100 kilometers further downstream by an important tributary also having its source in the Fouta Djalon, the Falémé River. At Bakel, 829 kilometers from its mouth and only 15 meters above sea level, the Senegal breaks through the ancient crystalline upland of the Boundou and enters the sedimentary central valley, more properly referred to as the Senegal River Valley. After passing the important valley river ports of Matam, Kaédi, Boghé, and Podor, the river leaves this valley to enter its delta region at Dagana, 194 kilometers from its mouth and at an elevation of only three meters. The river then flows past Richard-Toll and Rosso before entering the ocean 25 kilometers south of Saint Louis.

The flow and depth of the Senegal River are controlled almost entirely by the rains hitting the Fouta Djalon massif and their subsequent runoff, and only slightly by the rains and runoff in the semi-arid river region proper. With the beginning of the rainy season in Guinea in June, the floods usually reach Kayes early in July, reach their maximum depth towards the end of August, and subside in December. Owing to the very slight gradient of the river downstream from Bakel, the flood crest does not reach Dagana until the end of October. This annual flooding of the valley has two important effects upon the economy of the valley: it determines the period of navigation on certain stretches of the river and is indispensable in supplying silt and water for the valley farms.

Theoretically, navigation on the Senegal River is possible as far upstream as the Félou Rapids, a few kilometers upstream from Kayes, or a distance of close to 1,000 kilometers from its mouth. However, navigation conditions vary according to the section of the river and the period of the year. Navigation on the stretch of the river from its mouth to the Mafou sandbar (68 kilometers upstream from Podor) is controlled by the Keur Mour sandbar near Dagana, which permits a maximum draft of five meters during the low-water period. Thus, year-round navigation for ships drawing up to five meters is assured for a distance of 335 kilometers upstream from Saint Louis. Continuing upstream from Mafou, the river is strung with a series of sand and/or pebble bars which show above water during the low-water period, thus preventing all but the smallest native craft to pass, but which during the normal flood period are sufficiently covered to enable ships with drafts of up to three meters to penetrate as far as Kayes. Assured passage for vessels with maximum drafts of three meters is almost two months for Kayes and over two months for Matam and Kaédi. In addition, under unusually severe flood conditions, ships drawing up to five meters can penetrate

TABLE 35 Approximate Periods of Navigation on the Senegal River

Maximum Draft	Saint Louis to Mafou (335 km)	Mafou to Matam (288 km)	Matam to Kayes (301 km)
5 meters	All year	Occasional years	Occasional years
3 meters	All year	5 Aug.–15 Oct.	10 Aug.– 5 Oct.
2 meters	All year	25 July–20 Oct.	1 Aug.–10 Oct.
1 meter	All year	5 July–20 Nov.	15 July–10 Nov.

Sources: A. Mas, "Les Voies Navigables en A.O.F.," *A.O.F. Magazine* (Octobre 1955), p. 24, modified by Mission d'Aménagement du Fleuve Sénégal, *Situation Actuelle des Transports dans la Vallée du Fleuve Sénégal*, Bulletin No. 118 (Avril 1960), p. 8.

as far as Kayes, although usually for very short periods. It must be noted at this point, however, that the maximum permissible draft for ships crossing the sandbar at the mouth of the Senegal River varies from 2.4 to 3.6 meters—a severe handicap to full utilization of the river's potential.[15]

Scheduled service on the Senegal River is provided by the Société Anonyme des Messageries du Sénégal (MESSAGAL), which has a government monopoly between Saint Louis and Bakel, and by approximately 450 shallow-draft native canoes which ply the waters of the river between Saint Louis and Kayes. Only a small amount of freight is moved on the river in the course of a year. In 1965 only 19,496 tons of river cargo were recorded as having been loaded and unloaded at the port of Saint Louis, the port through which almost all the river cargo destined to or arriving from Dakar passes (see Table 36). This tabulation took into account only the cargo transported and/or recorded by MESSAGAL, and excluded most of the cargo manipulations of the small native haulers. Since these native canoes transport an estimated 5,000 tons of merchandise to Saint Louis and return with approximately twice that amount in the course of a year,[16] the port of Saint Louis handled approximately 35,000 tons of cargo in 1965, with total cargo movements on all stretches of the river for the same year probably not exceeding 50,000 tons. Because of the economic dormancy of the Senegal River Valley, the volume and nature of merchandise movements on the river have changed very little since independence. However, should plans for the economic rejuvenation of the valley materialize in the future, there will very probably be a marked increase in the movement of goods on the river. The creation of the Comité Inter-États pour l'Aménagement du Fleuve Sénégal in February 1964 by the riparian states of Senegal, Mauritania, Mali, and Guinea, and the subsequent grant of 5.8 million dollars by the United Nations Special Fund for studies of the river have been important steps to this end. Long-range plans call for the improvement of agriculture, the construction of irrigation, navigation, and power dams, and the improvement of existing transportation facilities, including the development of port facilities at Kayes in Mali and the construction of new facilities at Saint Louis for river traffic and for ocean-going vessels. Should these plans materialize, they will probably succeed in

TABLE 36   Recorded Senegal River Traffic Passing Through the Port of
Saint Louis for 1965

(*In Metric Tons*)

	Total	Total	Senegal Ports	Mauritanian Ports
Loaded				
Construction material	5,559		301	5,258
Sugar	4,403		264	4,139
Imported rice	2,211		638	1,573
Flour	875		249	626
Edible oil	768		98	670
Petroleum products	514		143	371
Other commodities	2,995		574	2,421
Total loaded		17,325	2,267	15,058
Unloaded				
Rice from Richard-Toll	1,085		1,085	. . .
Gum arabic	80		80	. . .
Millet	80		75	5
Other commodities	926		877	49
Total unloaded		2,171	2,117	54
Total loaded and unloaded		19,496	4,384	15,112
Passengers: From Saint Louis Up-River		1,815		
From Up-River to Saint Louis		9,807		
Total		11,622		

Source: Files of the Société Anonyme des Messageries du Sénégal, Saint Louis, Senegal.

diverting most of the overseas trade of the valley region from Dakar to Saint Louis, a loss not very considerable today but which could amount to an appreciable tonnage in the future.

The Niger River has its source in the Guinea Highlands near the border of Guinea and Sierra Leone, less than 250 kilometers from the ocean. Instead of flowing directly out to sea, however, it flows from Guinea into Mali, reaches a distance of 1,350 kilometers from the sea, and then turns back toward the ocean, passing through Niger, forming the frontier between Niger and Dahomey, and entering the Gulf of

FIG. 43   Loading the *Bou-el-Mogdad* at the Port of Saint Louis; it provides
scheduled cargo and passenger service between Saint Louis and Bakel

Guinea through Nigeria, 4,000 kilometers from its source. The unfortunate fact that this river has its lower course in formerly British territory and its main body in what were French lands has prevented its development of a major artery to interior West Africa, and has limited its development in former French West Africa as solely a route of internal communication. Like that of the Senegal River, its flow (as well as those of its principal tributaries, the Tinkisso, Milo, Niandan, Sankarani, and Bani rivers) is seasonally conditioned, with a consequent seasonal limitation on navigation. In addition, rapids preclude navigation along certain stretches of the river even during the period of high water. Within former French West Africa, there are the rapids of Sotuba and Kenié between Bamako and Koulikoro, and the rapids of Labbezenga just downstream from Ansongo near the Mali-Niger border.

In the upper reaches of the river, the first navigable stretch is that between Kouroussa, Guinea, and Bamako, Mali, a distance of 374 kilometers. In addition, the 130-kilometer stretch of the Milo River between Kankan, Guinea, and its juncture with the Niger is also open to navigation. These stretches, however, are navigable only between July and December, and only by small barges having maximum drafts of up to 0.9 meter. Consequently, under normal conditions these two upper reaches of the Niger system play minor roles in the trade pattern of West Africa. This is evidenced by the fact that less than 5,000 tons of goods, virtually all destined for local markets, are transported annually on these stretches. It is also very unlikely that either of these two stretches will be improved for navigation, since it is estimated that over seven billion francs CFA (28.6 million U.S. dollars) would have to be expended on the project, mainly for the construction of locks.[17] In this respect, note should be made once again of the possibility of the construction of a railroad between Bamako and Kouroussa, which would absorb most of this seasonal river traffic as well as divert some of the overseas trade of Mali from the port of Dakar to the port of Conakry.

The stretch of the middle Niger River between Koulikoro and Gao[18] is the most important one within Mali in terms of merchandise and passenger haulage. In 1959, the last "normal" year, approximately 60,-000 tons of recorded cargo moved on this stretch of the river, an estimated 48,000 tons between Koulikoro and Ségou, of which approximately 32,000 tons (mainly rice and cotton from the Office du Niger, millet, and peanuts) were debarked at Koulikoro. Approximately 16,000 tons (largely cement, salt, sugar, and petroleum derivatives) were embarked at the port.[19] However, as with freight movements on the Senegal River, the recorded movement of goods on the Niger River is less than the actual total, the difference being accounted for by small native haulers (approximately 20,000 tons annually). In 1963, with the direction of Mali's overseas trade diverted from the main axis of the Niger River and the Dakar-Niger Railroad to roads running perpendicular to this axis, 47,580 tons of freight were recorded as having moved on the river, of which 55 to 60 per cent consisted of millet and rice.[20] (Millet and rice traditionally account for 50 to 60 per cent of the cargo movements carried on this stretch of the river.) With the reopening of the rail line between Senegal and Mali on July 1, 1963, the general pattern of 1959 has generally been restored. The scheduled services on the river between Bamako and Kouroussa, Bamako and Kankan, and Koulikoro and Gao

are provided by the Compagnie Malienne de Navigation, the nationalized successor to the Société des Messageries Africaines. Service is provided by means of small river freighters, tugs, and barges, with the principal ports of call being Koulikoro, Ségou, Markala, Mopti, Niafounké,
Diré, and Gao.

The relatively low total volume of cargo moved on this central stretch
of the Niger River is attributable largely to the limited commercial pro-
ductivity of the immediate hinterland, a limitation imposed by the sahelian and dry savanna climates coupled with distance from the sea. In
addition, scheduled service on this stretch of the river is usually suspended from early March to mid June, while even during the height of
the navigation period the normal maximum permissible draft is only 1.7
meters, with variations occurring to the extent of the summer rains hitting the Guinea Highlands and the period of the year. Thus the Niger
River, like the Senegal River, has never fulfilled the great expectations
of the early colonial authorities. Because of factors of navigational difficulties, climatic limitations to the development of intensive commercial
agriculture, and distance from the sea, the Niger River, like the Senegal
River, plays a decidedly secondary role in helping to feed the port of
Dakar. Instead of being vital links in an integrated pattern of transportation as at first envisaged, these two rivers are today relatively unimportant indirect feeders of the port. Nevertheless, the Niger River is and
will continue to be, despite its limitations, an important internal avenue
of communication for landlocked Mali.

Thus the port of Dakar is connected to its hinterland directly by rail
and road and indirectly by river transportation. It is a transportation network that has been conditioned largely by the colonial past of the region
—that is, it is a network geared primarily to the evacuation of a few
primary resources coupled with strategic considerations. In areas where
the commercial economy is most intensively developed, the network is
the densest and road construction is more permanent; in remoter regions, the transportation web is much more rudimentary. In addition,
the pattern is such that it tends to drain this hinterland to the port of
Dakar (or to the secondary port of Kaolack) often at the expense of a
shorter and/or more economical outlet. Good examples of this are the
regions of Casamance and Sine-Saloum, both of which fall within the

pull of Dakar to varying degrees but which, under conditions not controlled by political factors, should naturally drain via the Gambia River.

However, with the dissolution of the Federation of French West Africa and the granting of individual territorial sovereignty, national interests are operating to modify greatly this long-established pattern. In Mauritania the construction of the new port at Port Étienne and the wharf at Nouakchott, coupled with the building of the MIFERMA Railroad and the extension and improvement of the road network, will eventually remove virtually all of the country from the Dakar hinterland. In landlocked Mali the recent political estrangement from Senegal dramatically pointed out the dangers inherent in virtual total dependence upon a single extranational maritime outlet, and steps are being undertaken to reduce this dependence. The construction of a rail line between Mali and Guinea is being weighed, while the road network between Mali and the neighbors to the south is being greatly improved. Also it is probable that in the near future the Gambia will federate with Senegal, thus further modifying the existing pattern by introducing a new and potentially powerful competitor to the port of Dakar for the trade of the western Sudan —the port of Bathurst.

Therefore, within the next decade or two, a new pattern will emerge, the net effect of which will be to reduce substantially the areal extent of the present-day hinterland and/or reduce the pull of the port of Dakar. It is very likely that once the political barrier between Senegal and the Gambia is removed, and the new ports and transportation lines are completed, the port of Dakar will lose most of Mauritania to Port Étienne and Nouakchott, will lose Casamance and much of Sine-Saloum and the Rip to Bathurst, and will compete with Bathurst and the Gulf of Guinea ports (particularly Abidjan and Conakry) for the trade of the middle Niger Valley.

5 / Transportation Links
with the Hinterland

A VERY poor network of internal communications was inherited by the European colonial powers in West Africa. It consisted of a primitive system of dirt trails and river transportation, and was geared to a limited interregional exchange of a few commodities, principally cola nuts, dried fish, salt, and cattle. Contact with the outside world was restricted to caravan routes across the Sahara to the Moslem nations of the north. In their stead the Europeans established coastal trading posts and, eventually, maritime ports. The result was a complete disruption of these traditional African trading routes. Today only a very insignificant portion of the extranational trade of the states of West Africa crosses the Sahara.[1] In general, the rule for the distribution of ports in former French West Africa (whose main trunk was in the Sudan but which had four protrusions reaching the Atlantic coast in Senegal-Mauritania, French Guinea, the Ivory Coast, and Dahomey) was based upon the following broad rule: a major port per coastal territory located at the marine terminal of a rail line connecting that port with at least one of the two principal internal water arteries, the Senegal and Niger rivers. It was felt that by such a basic utilization of these natural waterways, supported by railroads and subordinate feeder roads, the principal handicaps to the construction of a coordinated and efficient territorial transportation network (those of huge distances and a relatively sparse population) could be resolved. However, it was only in the case of the former Dakar-Niger Railroad and the port of Dakar (and only after the abandonment of the port of Saint Louis as the major outlet of Senegal) that complete fruition of one of these projects came about. Today the port of Dakar is connected to the Niger River by the leading to a quick turnaround time, and, since 1963, the new petroleum refinery at M'Bao all bode well for the future.

The combination of location and site plus the accidents of history have also contributed to the historically important role of the port of Dakar within West Africa; in fact, this combination of factors has enabled the port to play a role within colonial West Africa out of proportion to what it very probably should have played had the natural physical factors been the sole determinants. When the dusts of colonial conquest and annexation had settled, France, through conscious effort and design, became the leading colonial power in West Africa, leading, that is, in terms of total area under effective control. The Federation of French West Africa encompassed 76 per cent of the total area of politically determined West Africa. Avoiding the hostile Guinea Coast, the French consciously directed their efforts to consolidating their holdings from stations along the west coast of West Africa, especially in the setting up of a great east-west trunk artery from the coast at Saint Louis inland to the heart of the West African Sudan by using the Senegal and Niger rivers as the principal axis. Physical limitations to the use of the port of Saint Louis, however, soon dictated the shift of the base of operations to Dakar and the abandonment of the use of the Senegal River as part of the trunk artery, although the basic premise for the consolidation of French holdings along the east-west axis was retained. Thus Dakar became the focal point for the consolidation of French holdings in West Africa—the political, economic, commercial, and cultural capital for three-quarters of the land area of West Africa, a largely self-contained mass with very limited contacts with the other countries of West Africa. With this emphasis upon Dakar came a rapid development of Dakar and its institutions, a development geared to a very large extent to service all the French holdings in West Africa.

The port of Dakar developed within this framework. It developed a hinterland which encompassed all Senegal and virtually all former French Sudan and Mauritania. It became the focal point of the great trunk artery, of the road network within Senegal, of extra-Senegalese coastal cargo movements, and of Senegalese cabotage traffic. It also became an important outlet for the industries of the Cape Verde industrial complex, an industrial complex geared, to a large extent, to serving the needs of French West Africa, French Equatorial Africa, Togo, and Cameroon. To be sure, the port of Dakar did not develop in a vacuum; other ports developed in former French West Africa to help drain this extensive colonial holding as well as to provide local services. However, with the eventual exceptions of the ports of Abidjan in the Ivory Coast and Conakry in former French Guinea, these ports, in terms of facilities, cargo movements, and/or extent of hinterlands, could only be classified as secondary ports; the main emphasis, at least until the creation of the port of Abidjan in 1950, was upon the port of Dakar.

Complete political independence for the states of former French West Africa by the end of 1960 resulted in a disruption of the colonially induced pattern. No longer was there one monolithic French colonial holding which developed and existed to a very large extent separate and distinct from the rest of West Africa. There were now eight independent states of former French West Africa plus independent Liberia, Ghana, Togo, and Nigeria, each free to decide its own political and economic destiny. By 1965 Sierra Leone and the Gambia had joined this list. Although independence did not (and could not) mean an immediate and complete disruption of the colonially induced pattern established by the French, a new set of forces and factors has been introduced which has modified the old pattern somewhat and which is in the process of further changing the old colonially induced order. When these forces will have run full course, there will be a considerable modification in the pre-independence pattern. In the specific terms of this study, there will be a substantial modification in the role of the port of Dakar within independent West Africa.

The first important step in this direction occurred in August 1960 with the rupture of the Mali Federation, the severance of political and economic relations between Senegal and the new Republic of Mali, and the loss of the Mali hinterland to the port of Dakar for thirty-four months. During this period Mali developed new road ties with Upper Volta and the Ivory Coast (and consequently with the Abidjan-Niger Railroad). When political and economic relations between Mali and Senegal were restored early in 1963 and the former Dakar-Niger Railroad was reopened on July 1 of that year, the pre-independence pattern was not completely resumed. Landlocked Mali, no longer wishing to be virtually entirely dependent upon a single extranational outlet (Senegal) for her overseas commodity movements, consciously continued to use the newly developed outlets for approximately one-quarter to one-third of such movements. In addition, the possibility of constructing a rail link between the Mali Railroad at Bamako and the Guinea Railroad at Kouroussa or Kankan, and thus connecting Mali directly with the port of Conakry, is still open though remote at present owing to the factor of cost relative to economic value plus the present disrepair of the Guinea Railroad. The construction of this link would give Mali a third principal overseas outlet (in addition to the ports of Dakar and Abidjan) and still further dilute the dependence upon the port of Dakar.

Another factor forcing Mali to reduce her dependence upon the ports of Senegal is one of balance of payments difficulties. Mali has an unfavorable trade balance with Senegal, buying the services of the port of Dakar and the Senegal Railroad plus manufactured goods (such as cement) from the industries of the Cape Verde industrial complex. In return Mali sends Senegal cotton, rice, and miscellaneous agricultural commodities, though not enough to make up the cost difference. The principal export of Mali, live animals, finds a greater market in the wetter savanna and Guinean zones to the south, with a consequent favorable trade balance with the Ivory Cost and Upper Volta. Therefore, since independence there has been a strengthening of Mali's ties with these two countries, talk of improving ties with Guinea, and a loosening of the strong pre-independence, colonially induced ties with Senegal. Although the immediate effect of this is not apparent in an examination of the absolute movement of Malian cargo at the port of Dakar, a study of the overseas cargo movements to and from Mali shows the relative decrease of Mali's dependence upon the ports of Senegal and especially upon the port of Kaolack. In the future it is very likely that, while the absolute dependence may increase, the relative importance of the port of Dakar in the extra-African trade-movement pattern of Mali will remain considerably below the pre-independence level. Although most of Mali will continue to fall within the effective hinterland of the port of Dakar, independence (and especially the period of severed relations between Senegal and Mali) has had the apparently permanent effect of loosening Mali's ties with the port.

Unlike for Mali, where independence only loosened the country's ties with the port of Dakar, independence for Mauritania is in the process of virtually severing the historic relationship. Prior to independence almost all the imports into Mauritania passed through the port of Dakar. From Dakar they moved to Mauritania via one of four principal routes: (1) by rail to Saint Louis and then by road, river, or river and road to Mauritania; (2) by rail to Linguère and then by road to Mauritania; (3) by rail to Kayes and then by road to Mauritania; and (4) by coastal freighter to Port Étienne. With the exception of most of the smoked, dried, and salted fish moving directly out of Port Étienne to mainly African markets, virtually all the country's limited overseas exports moved out following a reverse pattern of the above routes.

The first important post-independence modification in this pattern came with the improvement of the port facilities at Port Étienne so that instead of only lighterage service being available for larger ships, direct accostage was made possible at the lighterage quay for ships drawing up to seven meters. In addition a mineral port and an iron-ore loading wharf with loading facilities were constructed to handle the ore exports from the Société Anonyme des Mines de Fer de Mauritanie (MIFERMA) operations at Fort Gouraud. The mineral and general-cargo ports are connected to the new MIFERMA Railroad which ties Port Étienne with Fort Gouraud and the Trans-Mauritania Highway. In April 1963 the first shipment of iron ore was made, with a total of 1,100,000 tons exported during that year. (By 1968 planned annual exports are to reach 7,500,000 tons.) In addition to moving the iron ore out, an agreement between MIFERMA and the Société Nationale des Transports Ferroviaires provides for the railroad to move two freight cars from and to the interior with each movement of an ore train. Thus the improvement of the port facilities and the construction of the MIFERMA Railroad have managed to create an effective hinterland for the port of Port Étienne, which is no longer limited to the immediate vicinity of the city but includes most of northern Mauritania. With future improvements in the facilities at the port and the eventual construction of a road connecting Port Étienne with the Trans-Mauritania Highway (today only a rudimentary trail connects Port Étienne with Nouakchott), the hold of Port Étienne on this region will be strengthened and lead to the virtual exclusion of direct movements from the port of Dakar. These will be largely limited to petroleum products from the refinery at M'Bao and the products of local Senegalese industries, although even these may eventually move almost entirely by coastal freighter to Port Étienne.

The new wharf at Nouakchott, completed in 1965, will have the eventual effect of removing most of central and southern Mauritania from the Dakar hinterland. However, the full effect of the wharf will not be felt until the present-day poor system of roads connecting Nouakchott with the rest of the country is improved. In this regard, the Four Year Development Plan (1963–1966) called for the bituminizing of the Trans-Mauritania Highway between Nouakchott and Rosso and for the improvement of the road system connecting Rosso with the cities and towns of southern Mauritania. The eventual though delayed completion of this phase of the plan plus similar improvements in the future should enable the wharf to draw most of the overseas traffic from central and southern Mauritania away from the port of Dakar. It is estimated that at first only 20,000 to 40,000 tons of cargo will be handled by the wharf, but that with the improvement of the road web and the eventual development of the copper ore deposits at Akjoujt, movements over the wharf should be close to 100,000 tons annually. It is the eventual copper operations that have furnished most of the economic justification for the construction of the wharf.

Thus independence and nationalism have combined to set into motion a series of forces which are in the process of virtually removing the Mauritanian hinterland from the port of Dakar, which will lose approximately 50 per cent of the areal extent of its hinterland but less than 10 per cent of the current volume of cargo handlings. As for Port Étienne, there was sufficient economic (as well as physical geographic) justification for the construction of the new mineral and general-cargo ports; the Fort Gouraud iron-ore deposits could not have been worked economically through the port of Dakar. The economic justification for the wharf at Nouakchott is more tenuous. The processed copper could very probably move economically from Akjoujt to the coast via the MIFERMA Railroad and Port Étienne either by a rail connection (as was planned originally) or by road. Economic nationalism, however, dictated the need for the wharf, and with it will come the virtual complete severance of the Mauritanian hinterland from the port of Dakar.

It is very unlikely that in the foreseeable future any portion of the Senegalese hinterland will be completely lost to the port of Dakar. There are, however, certain eventualities that could (and probably would) reduce the relative pull of the port in certain regions of the country. The first contingency is the economic future of the Senegal River Valley and the port of Saint Louis. Until June 1960 Saint Louis was officially a maritime port, but the combined effects of the difficulties of navigation on the lower reaches of the Senegal River (the present-day port is located 25 kilometers upstream from the river's mouth), the draft limitation of 2.4 to 3.6 meters imposed by the sandbar across the mouth of the river, the economic dormancy of the valley region, and the improvement of transportation links between Dakar and the valley region led to Saint Louis' disuse for maritime traffic. Today Saint Louis and the Senegal River Valley are completely within the pull of the port of Dakar.

Should the economic development plans for the valley materialize and the new port be constructed by cutting a channel through the sandbar that separates the port from the Atlantic Ocean (the lower course of the Senegal River runs parallel to the coast, being separated from the ocean by a narrow band of sand), the relative pull of the port of Dakar upon Saint Louis and the Senegal River Valley will very likely be reduced, since it is probable that some (or perhaps most) of the overseas movements to and from the valley will pass directly through the new port. An economic revival for the valley region should mean, on the other hand, an absolute increase in valley-oriented cargo movements at the port of Dakar, for although today all the extra-African movements to and from the valley region pass through Dakar, their total volume is slight. An economically rejuvenated valley region should lead to an absolute increase in the use of the port of Dakar as a transshipment center for water-borne movements to and from Saint Louis and other Senegal River ports and for continued movements by rail and road to Saint Louis and Matam.

The second contingency is the political future of independent Gambia and the status of the port of Bathurst. It is very probable that had the political fortunes of West Africa not led to the separate political development of the Gambia from that of Senegal, the Gambia River would have become the principal artery of French penetration of the West African

Sudan, and that near its mouth the equivalent to what is now the port of Dakar would have developed. The Gambia River and the site of the modern port of Bathurst have certain advantages for large-scale port development: (1) access to the port, which is located on the estuary of the river, is not encumbered by a sandbar across its mouth as occurs at many other West African ports, notably Saint Louis, Kaolack, and Ziguinchor (a depth of 8.2 meters exists at the entrance to the Gambia Estuary at low tide); (2) once the port of Bathurst is reached, adequate year-round protection is afforded from winds and swells; (3) ocean-going vessels drawing not more than 5.2 meters can penetrate 250 kilometers upstream as far as Kuntaur, which, along with Kaur and Balingho, is an upriver peanut-loading port; and (4) small vessels drawing up to two meters can reach Koina, approximately 500 kilometers upstream from Bathurst, throughout the year. Thus the Gambia River penetrates and is navigable within the heart of the Senegalese peanut country. The removal of the political and economic barrier between Senegal and the Gambia would open this river for the evacuation of the commercial peanut production of the Senegalese regions of Sine-Saloum, the Rip, and Casamance, as well as exert a strong pull on the limited commercial production of the Boundou and Mali. The immediate effect would very probably lead to the commercial decline (and eventual disuse) of the ports of Kaolack (as well as the secondary ports of the Saloum Estuary) and Ziguinchor, with new lines of communication in these regions leading to the Gambia River, whose port of Bathurst would most likely become one of the prime peanut-evacuation ports of West Africa. (On the basis of current production and evacuation statistics, annual peanut and peanut-derivative exports passing through the port of Bathurst would very probably exceed 200,000 tons.)

While this eventuality would almost certainly have a catastrophic effect upon the ports of Kaolack and Ziguinchor, its effect upon the port of Dakar would be much different. The closing of the port of Kaolack and the shifting of the main evacuation port of the regions of Sine-Saloum and the Rip further south would increase the effectiveness of the pull of the Senegal Railroad and the port of Dakar upon the peanut production in those subregions of Sine-Saloum now attracted equally by Dakar and Kaolack, with an increase in movements to the former port.

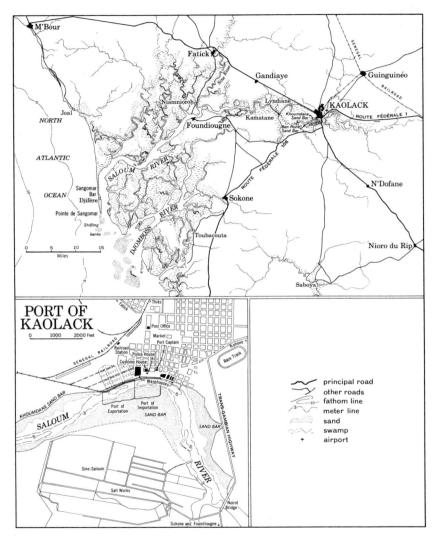

FIG. 44   Port of Kaolack

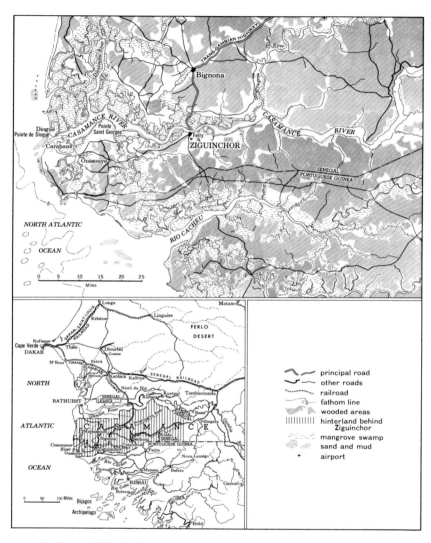

FIG. 45   Port of Ziguinchor

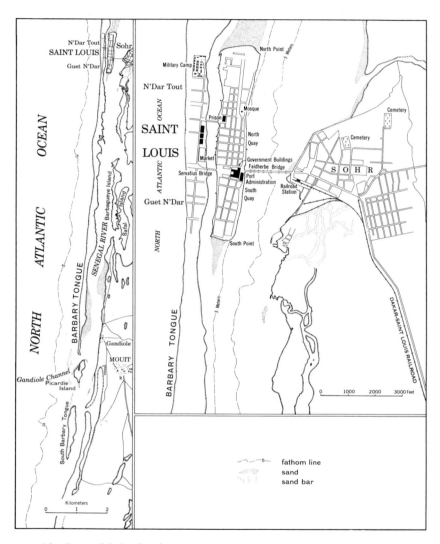

FIG. 46 Port of Saint Louis

In addition the exports of the SODEC peanut-oil plant at Lyndiane on the Saloum Estuary near Kaolack, which today move almost entirely down the estuary (83,058 tons of peanuts, peanut oil and peanut cake in 1963), would very probably move by rail to the port of Dakar. Thus, while free movement to the port of Bathurst would probably divert many of the overseas exports of the Boundou and Mali from Dakar (this could easily be done by constructing a 50-kilometer feeder road or railroad embranchment between Tambacounda on the Senegal Railroad and Koina on the Gambia River), this loss would be more than offset by the diversion to Dakar of over 100,000 tons of Sine-Saloum exports now moving down the Saloum Estuary.

However, an improved port of Bathurst would also succeed in becoming the principal feeder of Casamance as well as of the Gambia. While the Trans-Gambia Highway and the cabotage service between Dakar and Ziguinchor have managed to tie Casamance effectively to the Dakar hinterland today, this southern region of Senegal would very probably, under the eventuality of a Senegalese-Gambian union, fall largely within the Bathurst hinterland for incoming overseas movements as well as for exports, thus loosening the ties of Casamance to the Dakar hinterland for incoming extra-African cargo movements. In any event, independence for Senegal and the Gambia plus their probable eventual political and economic union should result in a reorientation of much of the overseas trade of Senegal and Mali to the greater benefit of the port of Bathurst and to a more limited extent to the port of Dakar. And it would probably sound the knell for the Senegalese secondary ports of Kaolack and Ziguinchor. It would also have the effect of largely removing one portion of Senegal—Casamance—which is today strongly within the pull of the port of Dakar (at least in terms of overseas imports) from the Dakar hinterland and tying it closely to the port of Bathurst, though it would still be dependent upon the industries of the Cape Verde industrial complex to satisfy some of its industrial needs.

It is the Cape Verde industrial complex that has so far felt the effects of independence the strongest. The post-World War II development of most of these industries was geared to a large extent to satisfy the needs of much of French-speaking Africa. This in turn was reflected in the cargo-handling mix at the port of Dakar, where extra-Senegalese African cargo embarkations from these industries comprised a relatively large percentage of the total cargo loaded at the port. No other city in French Africa came close to competing with Dakar in this field before independence, the factors of location, tradition, climate, and market leading to its rapid growth. Independence, however, has led to the development of competitive industries in traditional Senegalese markets, notably the Ivory Coast, and with this competition has come a marked decrease in intra-African industrial exports and their loadings at the port of Dakar. It is very unlikely that they will ever regain their pre-independence volume unless a true West African customs union develops; future exports appear to be limited to neighboring states.

Thus independence for virtually all West Africa (and for the eight territories of former French West Africa in particular) has had a strong effect upon the colonially induced role of the port of Dakar within this region. It has modified or is in the process of modifying the historic role of the port within West Africa by reducing the areal extent of its hinterland, by loosening the pull of the port on parts of its traditional hinterland, and by reducing the role of the port as a mover of industrial goods from the Cape Verde industrial complex. When the full effects of these changes have made themselves felt, the colonially induced role of the port of Dakar within West Africa will be substantially reduced. Although its relative role within West Africa will be decreased, the absolute volume of cargo moving through the port should increase as the conscious effort to develop and intensify the economy of Senegal begins to bear fruit, notably in increased peanut and phosphate exports. In the future Dakar will continue to be one of the world's great bunkering centers (at least until the era of nuclear-powered ships) and one of the more important ports of West Africa in terms of cargo and bunkering handlings, though sacrificing some of its former hinterland to other West African ports, notably Port Étienne, Nouakchott, Bathurst, Abidjan, and possibly Saint Louis and Conakry.

Notes

Introduction

1. With the exception of Senegal, the states of former French West Africa are technically no longer members of the French Community. However, with the exception of Guinea, all of the states retain close economic and cultural ties with France. Hence, for want of a better term, the name West African Community will be used in this study to refer collectively to those seven states retaining close ties with France.

2. Recognizing the importance of continued economic cooperation, the six states of former French West Africa remaining within the Community signed a convention on June 9, 1959, establishing the West African Customs Union (Union Douanière des États de l'Afrique de l'Ouest). Unfortunately, following the breakup of the Mali Federation and subsequent derogations on the part of member states, the total customs union originally envisaged has not yet materialized.

1 / The Physical Factors Conditioning the Development of the Port

1. Since 1960 Saint Louis is, at least temporarily, no longer a maritime port.

2. The term "Sudan" refers to the region of Africa lying between the semi-arid southern fringes of the Sahara and the humid equatorial climate to the south. It is characterized by a savanna (and possibly a wetter sahelian) climate and an open grasslands vegetation with scattered trees.

3. The hinterland of the port of Dakar as defined in this study (see Fig. 1) is delineated on the basis of points of origin of cargo debarkations and destinations of cargo embarkations at the port during 1966.

4. Port Autonome de Dakar, Service des Statistiques, *Statistiques Comparées: Mois de Décembre 1965,* p. 2.

5. *Ibid.*

6. The climatic divisions used by the writer are modifications drawn from two sources, either of which should be consulted for a detailed study of the climatic base of West Africa: (*a*) R. J. Harrison Church, *West Africa: A Study of the Environment and of Man's Use of it* (4th ed. rev.), pp. 21–90 and (*b*) Jacques Richard-Molard, *Afrique Occidentale Française* (3rd ed. rev.), pp. 14–50.

2 / The Historical Basis for the Growth and Development of the Port

1. A French naval officer who between 1838 and 1842 established trading posts along the Gulf of Guinea.

2. For further and more comprehensive studies of the historical development of West Africa, particularly in reference to former French West Africa, see: (*a*) Richard-Molard, *Afrique Occidentale Française*; (*b*) G. Brasseur, *L'A.O.F.*; (*c*) Edmond Séré de Rivières, *Le Sénégal-Dakar*; (*d*) André Villard, *Histoire du Sénégal*; and (*e*) Réné Sédillot, *Histoire des Colonisations.*

3. The term "Petite-Côte" refers to the coast of Senegal between Cape Verde Peninsula and the Saloum Estuary.

4. Georges Gabriel Ribot and Robert Lafon, *Dakar: Ses Origines, Son Avenir,* p. 10.

5. Claude Faure, *Histoire de la Presqu'île du Cap Vert et des Origines de Dakar,* pp. 114–15 (translated by the writer).

6. *Ibid.,* p. 115 (translated by the writer).

7. Villard, *Histoire du Sénégal,* p. 165 (translated by the writer).

3 / Port Facilities and Traffic

1. Interview with the port authorities.

2. Las Palmas, the principal bunkering competitor of Dakar, has a storage capacity of approximately 300,000 cubic meters.

3. Interview with the port authorities.

4. However, it was announced in February 1967 that Mali would rejoin the franc zone.

5. Port Autonome de Dakar, Services des Statistiques, *Statistiques Comparées: Mois de Décembre 1965.*

6. *Ibid.,* p. 13.

7. Interview with the port authorities.

8. Port Autonome de Dakar, Services des Statistiques, *Statistiques Comparées: Mois de Décembre 1965,* pp. 26–30.

9. *Ibid.*

10. *Ibid.*

11. The first stage of the new refinery (with an initial capacity of 600,000 tons per year) was put into operation in January 1964.

12. For the effect of the Trans-Gambia Highway on the movement of goods to and from Ziguinchor, see Chapter 5.

13. Port de Commerce de Dakar, *Renseignements Statistiques Comparés 1957,* p. 56.

4 / The Economic Hinterland

1. Owing to the importance of Dakar and Cape Verde Peninsula as conditioners of cargo movements at the port of Dakar, they will be examined separately from the rest of Senegal.

2. For a good recent study of the social aspects of the city of Dakar, see Assane Seck, *Dakar* (Faculté des Lettres et Science Humaines de Dakar: Travaux du Département de Géographie, No. 9) (Dakar: Université de Dakar).

3. This conference, convened in the capital city of former French Equatorial Africa, advanced the concept of greater African participation in colonial administration, and emphasized the need for economic reforms and development.

4. In addition to the six peanut-oil mills in Senegal, there is a small, state-owned one at Koulikoro in Mali which was rebuilt and reopened in 1964. It supplies only the local oil and soap market, with no exports planned.

5. The two soap-producing plants belong to HSOA and V. Q. Petersen, the latter exporting most of its oil but using some for local soap production. The traditional market for this soap is in Senegal, with some going to Mali and Mauritania. Virtually none passes through the port of Dakar.

6. For an excellent study of the economic impact of the peanut oil industry (and industrialization in general) upon the Senegalese economy see *Les Industries du Cap Vert* (Dakar: Institut de Science Économique Appliquée, 1964).

7. Note should be made of the importance of ports in conditioning the locational pattern of the Senegalese peanut-oil industry, the sole exception being the SEIB plant at Diourbel. However, in the cases of the SODEC and SEIC plants, added incentive is provided by their location in the productive peanut-producing regions of Sine-Saloum and Casamance, respectively.

8. Although the Convention of Association provided that commodity prices of the associated states were to be aligned with world market prices effective November 1, 1964, France and Senegal renewed their quota agreements to last at least until the 1965–1966 peanut year to safeguard Senegal against an abrupt fall in revenue.

9. Annual report of the Contrôle Financier du Sénégal, *La Campagne Arachidière 1963–1964 au Sénégal.*

10. A third, small mill, built in 1942, also exists at Dakar. However, it processes semolina, corn, and millet almost entirely for the local market, and has little effect on port cargo movements.

11. "Informations d'Outre-Mer," *Industries et Travaux d'Outremer,* 13ᵉ Année-No. 138 (Mai 1965), p. 362.

12. *Ibid.*

13. "Informations d'Outre-Mer," *Industries et Travaux d''Outremer,* 12ᵉ Année-No. 133 (Decembre 1964), p. 1059.

14. République du Sénégal, *Plan Quadriennal de Développement 1961– 1964,* p. 114 (translated by the writer).

15. *Les Industries du Cap Vert,* p. 30.

16. République du Sénégal, Ministère du Plan et du Développement, Service de la Statistique, *Bulletin Statistique et Économique Mensuel, Année 1966,* No. 5 et 6 (Mai–Juin 1966) (Dakar: Grande Imprimerie Africaine), p. 6.

17. "Développement Comparé des Industries Sénégalaises et Ivoiriennes," *Africa,* 6ᵉ Année, No. 31 (Avril/Mai 1964), pp. 35–41.

18. *Ibid.*

19. André Villard, *Histoire du Sénégal,* p. 82 (translated by the writer).

20. Georges Hardy, *La Mise en Valeur du Sénégal de 1817 à 1854,* p. 238 (translated by the writer). This book is an excellent study of the early, frustrating attempts by France to develop the economy of Senegal.

21. *Ibid.,* pp. 240–41 (translated by the writer).

22. *Ibid.,* p. 167 (translated by the writer).

23. *Ibid.,* p. 167 (translated by the writer).

24. *Ibid.,* p. 289 (translated by the writer).

25. André Villard, *Histoire du Sénégal,* pp. 160–61 (translated by the writer).

26. *Ibid.,* p. 191 (translated by the writer).

27. However, it should be remembered that the SEIB peanut-oil plant at Diourbel also drains to Dakar.

28. One study prepared by the government showed that in 1958–1959 the average family income for a farmer in the "basin arachidier"—that is, the main peanut growing region of Senegal—was 123,375 francs CFA (504 U.S. dollars), or twice that of a non-peanut-growing farm family in the north.

Although there is probably some question as to the accuracy of the figures, it does show the relative prosperity of the peanut farmers.

29. In the more remote regions of Senegal, such as the Boundou, commercial peanut cultivation developed only within 50 kilometers of the railroad.

30. The generally accepted coefficients of transformation are: (*a*) decorticated peanut to undecorticated peanut: 0.70–0.72; (*b*) unrefined peanut oil to undecorticated peanut: 0.336; (*c*) unrefined peanut oil to decorticated peanut: 0.48; and (*d*) unrefined peanut oil to decorticated peanut: 0.445.

31. A future use of the peanut shell will very probably be in the making of wallboard to be used for building purposes.

32. Under the terms of Senegal's association with the European Economic Community, French price supports were to end after the 1963–1964 peanut year. However, to prevent an abrupt loss of revenue to Senegal, France extended these agreements, though at slightly lower rates, to last at least until the 1965–1966 peanut year.

33. 245 francs CFA equals one U.S. dollar.

34. Contrôle Financier du Sénégal, *La Campagne Arachidière 1963–1964 au Sénégal,* pp. 29–30.

35. *Ibid.,* p. 30.

36. "Informations d'Outre-Mer," *Industries et Travaux d'Outremer,* 13ᵉ Année-No. 137 (Avril 1965), p. 292.

37. Interviews with authorities of SDRS, ORSTOM, and IRAT. For fine detailed studies of the Senegal River Valley and its problems, see: (*a*) the series of reports prepared by the United Nations Mission for the Study of the Senegal River Basin and (*b*) J-L. Boutillier, P. Cantrelle, J. Causse, C. Laurent, and Th. N'Doye, *La Moyenne Vallée du Sénégal.*

38. République du Sénégal, Ministère des Travaux Publics, de l'Urbanisme, de l'Habitat, et des Transports, Régie des Chemins de Fer du Sénégal, *Budget d'Exploitation—Exercice 1964–1965,* p. 4.

39. Christian Valantin, "L'Arachide Sénégalaise et le Marché Commun," *Afrique Magazine,* XXVIIème (Novembre 1963), p. 43.

40. Interview with TAIBA officials.

41. *Ibid.*

42. "Information d'Outre-Mer," *Industries et Travaux d'Outremer,* 13ᵉ Année-No. 140 (Juillet 1965), p. 609.

43. These statistics are almost entirely overseas movements; the intra-West African trade of live animals, dried fish, salt, rice, millet, etc. were not recorded.

44. Henri G. Irani, *Contribution à l'Étude des Transports au Mali,* Tome I, p. 13.

45. Interview with J. Krantz-Grandmougin, Director of the Chambre de Commerce d'Agriculture et d'Industrie de Bamako, Bamako, Mali.

46. République du Sénégal, Ministère des Travaux Publics, de l'Urbanisme, de l'Habitat, et des Transports, Régie des Chemins de Fer du Sénégal, *Budget de l'Exploitation—Exercice 1964–1965,* p. 5.

47. *Ibid.,* p. 4.

48. République du Mali, Ministère du Plan et de l'Économie Rurale, *Rapport sur le Plan Quinquennal de Développement Économique et Social de la République du Mali 1961–1965,* pp. 16–17.

49. "L'Essor du Mali," p. 18. (Mimeographed.)

50. Chambre de Commerce, d'Agriculture et d'Industrie de Bamako, *Éléments du Bilan Économique 1964* (Mars 1965), p. 115.

51. Interview with the Director of the Compagnie Transafricaine for Mali. (245 Malian francs equal one U.S. dollar.)

52. République du Sénégal, Ministère des Travaux Publics, de l'Urbanisme, et des Transports, Régie des Chemins de Fer du Sénégal, *Compte Rendu de Gestion 1964–65* (Thiès: Imprimerie Chemins de Fer, 1965), Table 12 bis.

53. Henri G. Irani, *Contribution à l'Étude des Transports au Mali,* Tome I, pp. 116 and 120.

54. For excellent detailed studies of the Office du Niger, see: (*a*) Georges Spitz, *Sansanding: Les Irrigations du Niger* and (*b*) "L'Office du Niger," *Notes et Études Documentaires,* No. 2,240 (12 Décembre 1956).

55. Files of the Régie des Chemins de Fer du Sénégal and the Société Anonyme des Messageries du Sénégal.

5 / Transportation Links with the Hinterland

1. For consideration given at one time to the development of a trans-Saharan French alternative to coastal outlets, see Georges Tuaillon, *L'Afrique Occidentale Française par l'Atlantique ou par la Sahara?*

2. The Régie des Chemins de Fer du Sénégal (and consequently the operating statistics) operates on a fiscal year from July 1–June 30.

3. Files of the Régie des Chemins de Fer du Sénégal.

4. The other divisions were the Région Conakry-Niger, the Région Abidjan-Niger, and the Région Benin-Niger.

5. 1959 is the last full year that the system acted as a single economic entity prior to the Senegal-Mali split in 1960. Although through rail service was restored on July 1, 1963, traffic has not yet returned fully to the pre-1960 pattern.

6. République du Sénégal, Ministère des Travaux Publics, de l'Urbanisme, de l'Habitat, et des Transports, Régie des Chemins de Fer du Sénégal, *Compte Rendu de Gestion, Année 1962–63* (Thiès: Imprimerie Chemins de Fer, 1963), Tableau No. 12.

7. Files of the Régie Fédérale des Chemins de Fer de l'Afrique Occidentale Française.

8. République du Sénégal, Ministère des Travaux Publics, de l'Urbanisme, de l'Habitat, et des Transports, Régie des Chemins de Fer du Sénégal, *Budget d'Exploitation—Exercice 1964–1965.*

9. The Société des Messageries Africaines has been nationalized by the independent Mali government, and is today known as the Compagnie Malienne de Navigation.

10. Interview with officials of the Régie Fédérale des Chemins de Fer de l'Afrique Occidentale Française.

11. République du Sénégal, Ministère des Travaux Publics, de l'Urbanisme, de l'Habitat et des Transports, Régie des Chemins de Fer du Sénégal, *Compte Rendu de Gestion, Année 1962–63* (Thiès: Imprimerie Chemin de Fer, 1963), p. 4.

12. République du Sénégal, Ministère des Travaux Publics, de l'Urbanisme et des Transports, Régie des Chemins de Fer du Sénégal, *Compte Rendu de Gestion 1964–65* (Thiès: Imprimerie Chemins de Fer, 1965), p. 2.

13. *Compte Rendu de Gestion, Année 1962–63,* p. 5.

14. See République du Mali, Ministère du Plan et de l'Économie Rurale, *Rapport sur le Plan Quinquennal de Développement Économique et Social de la République du Mali 1961–1965,* and B. Kusnetzov, "New Mali Railway," *New Africa,* Vol. 5, No. 6 (June 1963), p. 17.

15. For a very fine study of transportation on the Senegal River, see Mission d'Aménagement du Fleuve Sénégal, *Situation Actuelle des Transports dans la Vallée du Fleuve Sénégal,* Bulletin No. 118 (Avril 1960).

16. Chambre de Commerce de Saint-Louis-du-Sénégal et du Fleuve, *Brochure Tricentenaire de la Fondation de la Ville de Saint-Louis,* p. 41, and Mission d'Aménagement du Fleuve Sénégal, *Situation Actuelle des Transports,* p. 11.

17. Interview with officials of the Section de Navigation, Direction Hydrographique, Bamako, Mali.

18. Though navigable to Ansongo, no scheduled service is provided.

19. Files of the Section de Navigation, Direction Hydrographique, Bamako, Mali.

20. Files of the Compagnie Malienne de Navigation, Bamako, Mali.

Bibliography

PUBLIC DOCUMENTS

French West Africa

Gouvernement Général de l'Afrique Occidentale Française. *Statistiques Mensuelles du Commerce Extérieur de l'Afrique Occidentale Française, Commerce Spécial, Importations: Exportations Décembre 1939* (Gorée: Imprimerie du Gouvernement Général, 1940).

Gouvernement Général de l'Afrique Occidentale Française. *Statistiques du Commerce Extérieur de l'Afrique Occidentale Française, Commerce Spécial, Importations: Exportations, Année 1948* (Rufisque: Imprimerie du Gouvernement Général, 1949).

Haut Commissariat Général à Dakar, Études et Coordination Statistiques et Mécanographiques. *Bulletin Statistique et Économique Mensuel* (Avril 1959).

Régie Fédérale des Chemins de Fer de l'Afrique Occidentale Française. *Compte Rendu de Gestion Année 1958.*

Senegal

République du Sénégal. *Plan Quadriennal de Développement 1961–1964.*

République du Sénégal, Ministère des Travaux Publics, de l'Urbanisme, de l'Habitat et des Transports, Port de Commerce de Dakar, Section de la Statistique. *Trafic Général du Mois de Décembre 1963.*

République du Sénégal, Ministère des Travaux Publics et des Transports, Port de Commerce de Dakar. *Renseignements Statistiques Comparés 1962.*

République du Sénégal, Ministère des Finances et des Affaires Économiques, Service de la Statistique et de la Mécanographie. *Commerce Extérieur du Sénégal, Commerce Spécial, 12 Premier Mois 1963.*

République du Sénégal, Commissariat Général au Plan, Service de la Statistique et de la Mécanographie. *Bulletin Statistique et Économique,* Année 1962, No. 7 (Juillet 1962) (Dakar: Grande Imprimerie Africaine).

République du Sénégal, Ministère des Transports et des Télécommunications, Port de Commerce. *Statistiques Annuelles, 1961.*

République du Sénégal, Ministère du Plan et du Développement, Service de la Statistique. *Bulletin Statistique et Économique Mensuel,* Année 1963-No. 12 (Décembre 1963) (Dakar: Grande Imprimerie Africaine, 1964).

République du Sénégal, Ministère des Travaux Publics, de l'Urbanisme, de l'Habitat, et des Transports, Régie des Chemins de Fer du Sénégal. *Budget d'Exploitation—Exercice 1964–1965* (Thiès: Imprimerie Chemins de Fer, 1964).

République du Sénégal, Ministère des Travaux Publics, de l'Urbanisme, de l'Habitat et des Transports, Régie des Chemins de Fer du Sénégal. *Compte Rendu de Gestion, Année 1962–1963* (Thiès: Imprimerie Chemins de Fer, 1963).

République du Sénégal, Ministère du Plan et du Développement, Service de la Statistique. *Rapport Provisoire sur les Comptes de la Nation des Années 1959 à 1962* (Décembre 1963).

République du Sénégal, Ministère des Finances et des Affaires Économiques, Service de la Statistique et de la Mécanographie. *Situation Économique du Sénégal (1962).*

République du Sénégal, Ministère du Plan et du Développement, Service de la Statistique. *Commerce Extérieur du Sénégal, Commerce Spécial, 12 Premiers Mois 1965.*

République du Sénégal, Ministère du Plan et du Développement, Service de la Statistique. *Bulletin Statistique et Économique Mensuel,* Année 1966, No. 5 et 6 (Mai–Juin 1966) (Dakar: Grande Imprimerie Africaine, 1966).

République du Sénégal, Ministère des Travaux Publics, de l'Urbanisme et des Transports, Régie des Chemins de Fer du Sénégal. *Compte Rendu de Gestion 1964–65* (Thiès: Imprimerie Chemins de Fer, 1965).

Chambre de Commerce, d'Agriculture et d'Industrie de Dakar. *L'Économie du Sénégal* (2ème Édition) (Juillet 1965).

Chambre de Commerce, d'Agriculture et d'Industrie de Dakar. *L'Économie du Sénégal* (Avril 1961).

Chambre de Commerce de Saint-Louis-du-Sénégal et du Fleuve. *Brochure Tricentenaire de la Fondation de la Ville de Saint-Louis* (Saint Louis: Chambre de Commerce de Saint-Louis-du-Sénégal et du Fleuve, 1959).

Contrôle Financier du Sénégal. *La Campagne Arachidière 1963–1964 au Sénégal.*

Contrôle Financier du Sénégal. *La Campagne Arachidière 1961–1962 au Sénégal.*

Contrôle Financier du Sénégal. *La Campagne Arachidière 1965–1966 au Sénégal.*

Port de Commerce de Dakar. *Renseignements Statistiques Comparés 1957* (Rufisque: Imprimerie du Haut Commissariat, 1958).

Port Autonome de Dakar, Service des Statistiques. *Statistiques Comparés: Mois de Décembre 1965.*

Mission d'Aménagement du Fleuve Sénégal. *Situation Actuelle des Transports dans la Vallée du Fleuve Sénégal,* Bulletin No. 118 (Avril 1960).

Mali

Ministère d'État Chargé du Plan et de la Coordination des Affaires Économiques et Financières, Direction de la Statistique. *Annuaire Statistique 1963 de la République du Mali.*

République du Mali, Ministère du Plan et de l'Économie Rurale. *Données Économiques.*

République du Mali, Ministère du Plan et le l'Économie Rurale. *Rapport sur la Plan Quinquennal de Développement Économique et Social de la République du Mali 1961–1965.*

République du Mali, Ministère d'État Chargé du Plan et de la Coordination des Affaires Économiques et Financières, Service de la Statistique Générale et de la Comptabilité Économique Nationale. *Bulletin Mensuel de Statistique,* No. 1 (Janvier–Février 1966).

République du Mali, Ministère d'État Chargé du Plan et de la Coordination des Affaires Économiques et Financières, Service de la Statistique Générale et de la Comptabilité Économique Nationale. *Statistiques du Commerce Extérieur (Commerce Spécial) 1965.*

République du Mali, Ministère d'État Chargé du Plan et de la Coordination des Affaires Économiques et Financières, Service de la Statistique Générale et de la Comptabilité Économique Nationale. *Bulletin Annuel de Conjuncture* (Avril 1963).

Ambassade de la République du Mali aux U.S.A. *L'Essor du Mali.*

Chambre de Commerce, d'Agriculture et d'Industrie de Bamako. *Éléments du Bilan Économique 1963* (Mai 1964).

BOOKS AND PERIODICALS

"L'Afrique d'Expression Française et Madagascar," *Europe-France Outremer,* 42ᵉ Année-No. 421 (Février 1965), 264 pp.

Boutillier, J-L., P. Cantrelle, J. Causse, C. Laurent, and Th. N'Doye. *La Moyenne Vallée du Sénégal.* Paris: Presses Universitaires de France, 1962.

Brasseur, G. *L'A.O.F.* Dakar: Institut Français d'Afrique Noire, 1957.

Capet, Marcel. *Les Économies d'A.O.F.* Paris: Librairie Générale de Droit et de Jurisprudence, 1958.

Church, R. J. Harrison. *West Africa: A Study of the Environment and of Man's Use of it.* London: Longmans, Green & Co., Ltd., 1963.

"Développement Comparé des Industries Sénégalaises et Ivoiriennes," *Africa,* 6ᵉ Année, No. 31 (Avril/Mai 1964), pp. 35–41.

"L'Évolution Économique du Sénégal," *Notes et Études Documentaires,* No. 3,054 (13 Janvier 1964), 49 pp.

Faure, Claude. *Histoire de la Presqu'île du Cap Vert et des Origines de Dakar.* Paris: E. Larose, 1914.

Fromont, Philippe. *Les Transports dans les Économies Sous-Développées: Problème des Investissements.* Paris: Librairie Générale de Droite et de Jurisprudence, 1957.

Guid'Ouest Africain 1962–1963. Paris: Diloutremer, 1962.

Hardy, Georges. *La Mise en Valeur du Sénégal de 1817 à 1854.* Paris: Emile Larose, 1921.

"Informations d'Outremer," *Industries et Travaux d'Outremer,* Janvier 1964– Juillet 1965.

Kuznetzov, B. "New Mali Railway," *New Africa,* Vol. 5, No. 6 (June 1963), p. 17.

Mas, A. "Les Voies Navigables en A.O.F.," *A.O.F. Magazine* (Octobre 1955), pp. 22–25.

"L'Office du Niger," *Notes et Études Documentaires,* No. 2,240 (12 Décembre 1956), 51 pp.

"Le Plan Quadriennal de la Mauritanie (1963–1966)," *Industries et Travaux d'Outremer,* 12ᵉ Année-No. 132 (Novembre 1964), pp. 959–968.

Poquin, Jean-Jacques. *Les Relations Économiques Extérieures des Pays d'Afrique Noire de l'Union Française 1925–1955.* Paris: Librairie Armand Colin, 1957.

"Le Premier Plan de Développement de la République du Sénégal (1961– 1962)," *Notes et Études Documentaires,* No. 2,911 (6 Août 1962), 58 pp.

"La République Islamique de Mauritanie," *Notes et Études Documentaires,* No. 2,687 (29 Juillet 1960), 50 pp.

"La République du Mali," *Notes et Études Documentaires,* No. 2,739 (13 Janvier 1961), 65 pp.

"La République du Sénégal," *Notes et Études Documentaires,* No. 2,754 (22 Février 1961), 48 pp.

Ribot, Georges Gabriel, and Robert Lafon. *Dakar: Ses Origines, Son Avenir.* Bordeaux: Imprimerie de G. Delmas, 1908.

Richard-Molard, Jacques. *Afrique Occidentale Française.* 3ème. ed. revue. Paris: Éditions Berger-Levrault, 1956.

Sedillot, Réné. *Histoire des Colonisations.* Paris: Librairie Arthème Fayard, 1958.

Séré de Rivières, Edmond. *Le Sénégal-Dakar.* Paris: Éditions Maritimes et Coloniales, 1953.

Spitz, Georges. *Sansanding: Les Irrigations du Niger.* Paris: Société d'Éditions Géographiques, Maritimes et Coloniales, 1949.
Tuaillon, Georges. *L'Afrique Occidentale Française par l'Atlantique ou par le Sahara?* Paris: Charles-Lavauzelle & Cie., 1936.
United States Department of the Army. Foreign Areas Studies Division. *U.S. Army Area Handbook for Senegal.* Washington: Department of the Army, 1963.
Valantin, Christian. "L'Arachide Sénégalaise et le Marché Commun," *Afrique Magazine,* XXVIIème (Novembre 1963), pp. 41–44.
Villard, André. *Histoire du Sénégal.* Dakar: Maurice Viale, 1943.
Wernstedt, Frederick L. *World Climatic Data: Africa.* State College: Pennsylvania State University.
West African Directory. London: Thomas Skinner & Co. (Publishers) Ltd., 1966.

REPORTS

Chambre de Commerce, d'Agriculture et d'Industrie de Bamako. *Éléments du Bilan Économique 1964* (Mars 1965).
Institut de Science Économique Appliquée. *Les Industries du Cap Vert.* Dakar: Institut de Science Économique Appliquée.
Irani, Henri G. *Contribution à l'Étude des Transports au Mali,* Tome I (Bamako: Ministère des Transports et Télécommunications, 1962).
Office du Niger-Délégation au Paysannat. *Organisation des Associations Cooperatives Agricoles.* Ségou: Office du Niger, 1958.
L'Office du Niger. Ségou: Office du Niger.
Poliakoff, M. J. *Le Traitement des Graines Oléagineuses.* Paris: Institut de Recherches pour les Huiles & Oléagineux.
Seck, Assane. *Dakar.* Dakar: Faculté des Lettres et Sciences Humaines de l'Université de Dakar (Travaux du Département de Géographie, No. 9).

Mauritania

République Islamique de Mauritanie, Service de la Statistique. *Bulletin Statistique et Économique,* No. 1 (Janvier 1964).
République Islamique de Mauritanie, Service de la Statistique. *Bulletin Statistique et Économique,* No. 2 (Numéro Spécial) (Mai 1964).

Other

République de Côte d'Ivoire, Ministère des Finances, des Affaires Économiques et du Plan, Direction de la Statistique, des Études Économiques et Démographiques. *Bulletin Mensuel de Statistique,* 19è Année, No. 6 (Juin 1966).

United States Department of Agriculture, Foreign Agricultural Service. *Fats, Oils, and Oil Seeds,* FFO 8–66 (July 1966).

United States Department of the Interior. *Phosphate Rock,* Preprint from the Bureau of Mines Minerals Yearbook, prepared by Richard W. Lewis (Washington, 1966).

Index